Lesbians and Gays and Sports

ISSUES IN LESBIAN AND GAY LIFE

Lesbians and Gays and Sports

PERRY DEANE YOUNG

MARTIN DUBERMAN
General Editor

CHELSEA HOUSE PUBLISHERS
New York 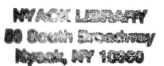 Philadelphia

I would like to thank Jim Baxter, publisher, and the rest of the staff at the *Front Page* in Raleigh, N.C., especially Rob Faggart, Paul Falduto, and Beth Harrison. Since October 1979, they have provided a serious and reliable forum for gays and lesbians in North and South Carolina. They not only provided me with current information through their computer networks, they also opened up a treasure trove of 25 years of gay history boxed up in their back room, including a complete file of the *Advocate,* our paper of record during this historic time.

CHELSEA HOUSE PUBLISHERS

EDITORIAL DIRECTOR   Richard Rennert
EXECUTIVE MANAGING EDITOR   Karyn Gullen Browne
COPY CHIEF   Robin James
PICTURE EDITOR   Adrian G. Allen
ART DIRECTOR   Robert Mitchell
MANUFACTURING DIRECTOR   Gerald Levine
ASSISTANT ART DIRECTOR   Joan Ferrigno

ISSUES IN LESBIAN AND GAY LIFE
SENIOR EDITOR   Sean Dolan
SERIES DESIGN   Basia Niemczyc

Staff for **LESBIANS AND GAYS IN SPORTS**
ASSISTANT EDITOR   Annie McDonnell
PICTURE RESEARCHER   Sandy Jones

Introduction © 1994 by Martin Duberman.

First Printing

1 3 5 7 9 8 6 4 2

Library of Congress Cataloging-in-Publication Data

Young, Perry Deane.
Lesbians and gays and sports/Perry Deane Young.
p. cm.—(Issues in lesbian and gay life)
Includes bibliographical references and index.
ISBN 0-7910-2611-6
      0-7910-2951-4 (pbk.)
1. Gays and sports. I. Title. II. Series.   93-43170
GV708.8.Y68 1994   CIP
796'.08'664—dc20   AC

FRONTISPIECE: Gay sprinters head for the finish line at Gay Games III.

▣ *Contents* ▣

How Different? *Martin Duberman*   7

1   GAYS AND SPORTS   13

2   WOMEN, SPORTS, AND THE L WORD   25

3   FOOTBALL   41

4   THE NATIONAL PASTIME   61

5   TENNIS   81

6   THE OLYMPICS   107

7   GAY ALTERNATIVES   121

Further Reading   141

Index   142

◈ *Issues in Lesbian and Gay Life* ◈

AFRICAN-AMERICAN LESBIAN AND GAY CULTURE
AIDS AND OTHER HEALTH ISSUES
ASIAN-AMERICAN LESBIAN AND GAY CULTURE
COMING OUT
ETIOLOGY: WHY ARE PEOPLE GAY OR STRAIGHT?
GROWING UP LESBIAN OR GAY
HOMOPHOBIA
LATIN-AMERICAN LESBIAN AND GAY CULTURE
LESBIAN AND GAY COMMUNITIES
LESBIAN AND GAY COUPLES AND PARENTING
LESBIAN AND GAY CULTURE
LESBIAN AND GAY LITERATURE
LESBIAN AND GAY PROTEST AND POLITICS
LESBIANS AND GAYS IN OTHER CULTURES
LESBIANS AND GAYS AND SPORTS
LESBIANS AND GAYS IN THEATER AND FILM
LESBIANS AND GAYS IN THE HOLOCAUST
LESBIANS AND GAYS IN THE MEDIA
LESBIANS AND GAYS IN THE MILITARY
LESBIANS, GAYS, AND PSYCHOLOGY
LESBIANS, GAYS, AND SPIRITUALITY
LESBIANS, GAYS, AND THE LAW
LESBIANS, GAYS, AND THE WORLD OF BUSINESS
NEITHER MALE NOR FEMALE: THIRD-GENDER FIGURES
RACE AND CLASS IN THE LESBIAN AND GAY WORLD
RECLAIMING THE LESBIAN AND GAY PAST: THE ANCIENT
    WORLD
RECLAIMING THE LESBIAN AND GAY PAST: THE UNITED STATES
TRANSVESTITES AND TRANSSEXUALS

Other titles in preparation

How Different?

MARTIN DUBERMAN

Just how different *are* gay people from heterosexuals? Different enough to support the common notion that they form a subculture—a shared set of group attitudes, behaviors and institutions that set them distinctively apart from mainstream culture? Of course the notion of the "mainstream" is itself difficult to define, given the many variations in religion, region, class, race, age and gender that in fact make up what we call "the heartland." And the problems of definition are further confounded when we broaden the discussion—as we should—from the context of the United States to a global one.

The question of the extent of "differentness"—of "queerness"—is subject to much debate, within as well as without the lesbian and gay world, and there are no easy answers for it. On one level, of course, all human beings share commonalities that revolve around basic needs for nurturance, affiliation, support and love, and those commonalities are so profound that they dwarf the cultural differences that set people apart.

Besides, it often isn't clear precisely what differences are under scrutiny. If we confine the discussion to erotic and affectional preference, then gay people are obviously different because of their primary attraction to members of their own gender. But what more, if anything, follows from that? Gay conservatives tend to believe that nothing follows, that aside from the matter of erotic orientation, gay people are "just folks"—just like everyone else.

But gay radicals tend to dispute that. They insist gay people have had a special history and that it has induced a special way of looking at the world. The radicals further insist that those middle-class gay white men who *deny* that their experience has been unusual enough to differentiate them from the mainstream are suffering from "false consciousness"—that they *are* more different—out of bed, as well as in—than they themselves would like to admit.

If one asked the average person what it is that sets gay men and lesbians apart, the likely answer would be that gay men are "effeminate" and lesbians "butch." Which is another way of saying that they are not "real" men or "real" women—that is, that they do not conform to prescribed cultural norms in regard to gender. It is true, historically, that "fairies" and "dykes" *have* been the most visible kind of gay person (perhaps because they were unable to "pass"), and over time they became equated in the popular mind with *all* gay people.

Yet even today, when gay men are often macho-looking body-builders and "lipstick" lesbians playfully flaunt their stereotypically feminine wiles, it can still be argued that gay people—whatever behavioral style they may currently adopt—are, irreducibly, gender nonconformists. Beneath many a muscled gay body still lies an atypically gentle, sensitive man; beneath the makeup and the skirts often lies an unusually strong, assertive woman.

This challenge to conventional gender norms—a self-conscious repudiation on the part of lesbian/gay radicals—is not a minor thing. And the challenge is compounded by the different kinds of relationships and families gay people form. A typical gay male or lesbian couple does *not* divide up chores, attitudes, or desire according to standard bi-polar "husband" and "wife" roles. Gay couples are usually two-career households in which an egalitarian sharing of rights and responsibilities remains the ideal, and often even the practice. And more and more gay people (particularly lesbians) are making the decision to have and raise children—children who are not trained to look to daddy for discipline and mommy for emotional support.

All this said, it remains difficult to *specify* the off-center cultural attitudes and variant institutional arrangements of lesbian and gay life. For one thing, the gay world is an extremely diverse one. It is not at all clear how much a black lesbian living in a small southern town has in common with a wealthy gay male advertising executive in New York City—or a transgendered person with either.

Perhaps an analogy is useful here. Literary critics commonly and confidently refer to "the Jewish novel" as a distinctive genre of writing. Yet when challenged to state *precisely* what special properties set such a novel apart from, say, a book by John Updike, the critics usually fall back on vague, catchall distinctions—like characterizing a "Jewish" novel as one imbued with "a kind of serious, kvetschy, doom-ridden humor."

Just so with any effort to compile an exact, comprehensive listing of the ways in which gay and lesbian subcultures (and we must always keep in mind that they are multiple, and sometimes at odds) differ from mainstream patterns. One wag summed up the endless debate this way: "No, there is no such thing as a gay subculture. And yes, it has had an enormous influence on mainstream life." Sometimes, in other words, one can *sense* the presence of the unfamiliar or offbeat without being able fully to articulate its properties.

Even if we could reach agreement on whether gay male and lesbian culture(s) stand marginally or profoundly apart from the mainstream, we would then have to account for those differences. Do they result from strategies adapted over time to cope with oppression and ghettoization? Or are they centrally derived from some intrinsic, biological subset—a "gay gene," for example, which initially creates an unconventional kind of person who then, banding together with likeminded others, create a novel set of institutional arrangements?

This interlocking series of books, *Issues in Lesbian and Gay Life,* is designed to explore the actual extent of "differentness" from mainstream values and institutions. It presents detailed discussions on a wide range of gay and lesbian experience and expression—from marriage and parenting, to history and politics, to spirituality and theology. The aim is to provide the reader with enough detailed, accurate information so that he or she can come to their own conclusions as to whether or not lesbian and gay subculture(s) represent, taken in their entirety, a significant departure from mainstream norms.

Whatever one concludes, one should always remember that differentness is not a disability nor a deficiency. It is another way, not a lesser way. Indeed, alternate styles of seeing (and being) can breathe vital new life into traditional forms that may have rigidified over time. Variant perspectives and insights can serve all at once to highlight the narrowness of conventional mores—*and* present options for broadening and re-vivifying their boundaries.

❖   ❖   ❖

On the night of June 18, 1994, my spouse and I went to the opening ceremonies of Gay Games IV in Columbia University's Wien Stadium. Eli is not remotely a sports fan, and I am only an intermittent one. I love watching tennis (during high school I was an avid team member); but also, the final rounds of any sporting event can arouse my competitive instincts, and the pageantry involved in special occasions like the Olympics can evoke my dramatic ones.

But the opening ceremonies of Gay Games IV proved exhilarating beyond all our expectations. The weather was steamy, the benches hard, and the sound system spotty. But all came to rights as the procession of athletes entered the stadium—thousands upon thousands in colorful array from some 50 countries, waving flags, ecstatically cheering the spectators and each other. We found ourselves yelling our lungs out like the stereotypic fans we thought we were not.

True, the Gay Games are based on an Olympic sporting model that glorifies "wholesome" bodies, emphasizes the importance of competition and winning, and reinforces normative gender roles. But gay and lesbian athletes do all that with a difference—and the difference is the saving grace. *Anyone* who wants to participate in the Gay Games is welcome to do so; and a fair number of the would-be warriors looked charmingly out of shape (and at least one of the male athletes I spotted wore a fetching pleated white skirt).

Besides, as several of the speakers at the 1994 opening ceremonies emphasized, the Gay Games are designed to *de*-emphasize rivalry in the name of unity. The speakers made moving (if perhaps sweetly utopian) reference to the primary importance of striving for and celebrating "a personal best" in performance—not to "beating" anyone else. This is what it could be like, I thought to myself that night in Wien Stadium, if straight America would only open itself up to the genuinely different and life-enhancing perspective that gay men and lesbians have to offer—and not only in the realm of sports.

The gay and lesbian athletes who compete in the Gay Games often describe the experience as a transformative one for them as individuals: they speak eloquently of the joy of being *wholly* who they are, and of joining hands with a circle of comrades. Yet it remains true that participation in sports will not by itself produce needed social change; that comes primarily from political organizing, commitment, and struggle. Getting the general public to see that some gay people can excel in sports of every kind, from bodybuilding to swimming, is not the equivalent of winning acceptance for the vast majority of gays and lesbians who are not particularly interested in or skilled at athletics.

Sports does make its contribution. It does change stereotypic views of who gay men and lesbians are and what they're capable of; it extends the range of representation of lesbian/gay life and gives a glimpse into the true diversity of our people. In doing so, it changes at least some mainstream attitudes, and that in turn leads, over time, to changes in laws and in legal opinions.

Perry Deane Young, in this engaging and often eloquent book, traces not only the history of gays and lesbians in sports but the deeply ingrained prejudice which has for so long kept many of us from participating (or even *wanting* to participate) in school or professional athletics—and kept the minority who did from revealing the actual nature of their sexual orientation. Though conditions have today improved *somewhat,* the official sports establishment continues to mock the very notion of a *gay* athlete as a contradiction in terms. And it continues rigidly to keep from the public any knowledge of the fact that some of our most prominent athletes have been, and continue to be, gay men and lesbians (even if most of those athletes are still too fearful to acknowledge the fact).

But as Perry Deane Young suggests, "What is clearly a new day in the history of gay people will perhaps also mark a new beginning for sports."

1

Gays and Sports

UNTIL RECENTLY, THE WORDS "homosexuals" and "sports" could not be spoken in the same sentence without arousing general disbelief, laughter, or even anger. The author of this book is painfully aware of that sad fact. In 1976, I signed a contract to write a book with David Kopay, who remains the only professional football player ever to talk openly about his homosexuality. Even my closest, well-meaning friends would burst out laughing when I explained the subject of the book I was working on: a gay pro football player. "I'm sorry," they would say, "but it's just the image of those two—gays and football players. It *is* funny." Even today, such reactions are more commonplace than they ought to be. In April 1993, Michelle Kaufman did an extensive series on gays and lesbians in sports for the *Detroit Free Press*. Except for one pro basketball player, every player she interviewed "snickered" when she first mentioned the subject.

David Kopay was never more than a journeyman running back during almost a decade in the National Football League (NFL). He did achieve one major distinction, however: Kopay was the first professional athlete in the history of American sports to publicly proclaim that he or she was a homosexual.

The idea of a gay football player contradicts two deeply held stereotypes about homosexuals and about athletes. Even after the social and sexual revolutions of the 1960s, the sports establishments fiercely guard and defend these images because many of them feel the very life—particularly the economic life—of their sports depends on it.

We learn to play before we learn to speak. Almost before our eyes are able to focus, an adult is likely to try to attract our attention by shaking a rattle or waving a toy of some sort. Particularly if the child is a boy, some of the first toys he is given are likely to be child-size versions of sports equipment: balls and bats and rackets and so on that his parents hope he will learn to use, for playing such games and achieving some measure of athletic success is regarded as an important rite of masculine passage in many households and schools. Those boys who do not, later on, show the requisite amount of interest in such sporting activities are liable to suffer the rough scorn of their peers and perhaps even their parents.

Until the most recent decades, when one spoke of sports, one spoke of boys and men. Little girls were expected to behave like young ladies at all times—and young ladies were not supposed to perspire. A young girl who did play ball with the boys was likely to be called a tomboy—nothing serious at a young age, but a potential cause for concern if she continued to dress and act like a boy beyond puberty.

Little boys who showed no interest in sports were sometimes looked on with serious concern. They might be regarded as shy, regressive, antisocial, unmanly—and more than a few million dollars in psychiatrists' fees have been wasted by worried parents trying to make sure that Junior "fit in."

And yet there is a grand tradition of boys and girls who did not fit in but became great artists or writers, their very genius testimony to the fact that they did not fit a mold, were too sensitive to be typecast. Their aberrant or "deviant" behavior came to be tolerated because of their artistic genius, but these, of course, were the exception. Who knows how many other males, different but with no particular talent to distinguish them, were harmed because they were not interested in or good at sports and thus did not conform socially? Who knows how many other females did not develop their athletic talent, at what expense to their individual development, because of fear of being perceived as unfeminine?

It took the new openness that followed the sexual revolution of the 1960s to create awareness of yet another group of men and women trapped by the stereotypes that surround athletics. These were the ones who were interested in sports and possessed sufficient physical ability to compete, but who knew in their hearts that they would be dismissed and ostracized if anybody ever learned that they were homosexual. They lived in a fierce daily fear of being found out that was just as bad as, if not worse than, that experienced by those who, by society's standards, were insufficiently or overly interested—"sissies" and "tomboys"—in sports.

While we have some records of homosexual artists in the centuries between the civilizations of ancient Greece and modern America, we have almost nothing available on homosexual athletes. For one thing, sports—at least from the time the "pagan" Olympic games were suppressed in A.D. 393 by the Christian emperor Theodosius the Great to the renewal of the modern Olympics in 1896—were just not that important in many societies. The figure of the athletic hero—in the sense of a person known and celebrated by an entire society for his or her sporting prowess—is by and large an invention of the 20th century, tied to the rise of the mass media and modern conceptions of leisure time. Although there are no records to prove it, we can assume that a certain percentage of sports figures throughout history have been homosexual, simply because, as Alfred Kinsey said so well in his pioneering study of male sexuality in 1949, "homosexuality has been a part of man's capacity since the dawn of mankind."

One of the chief complaints about sports in America is that their competitive aspects are overemphasized, particularly as regards young people. Connie Toverud, a high school guidance counselor from North Carolina, is one of many who believe that the win-or-nothing elitism of sports is wrong for the individual, wrong for society.

"In our society, somewhere between ages 13 and 15, sports become reserved for the elite. The athletically gifted play on the varsity and junior varsity teams. The talented play on club or recreation league teams, and the rest don't play. The idea of playing for fun and personal growth gets lost."

Writing in the *Chapel Hill [N.C.] Herald,* Toverud recalled a touching scene she witnessed during a faculty-student touch football game at one school where she taught:

"The students, naturally, were anxious to beat the faculty, and both teams were playing hard. Towards the end of the second half, the students' coach sent in Jim, whose turn it was to play. Jim was an autistic 17-year-old, uncoordinated and with a poor grasp of the rules of the game.

"The student quarterback (I'll call him Dave) was a troubled and angry young man who tried to hide his low self-esteem by dominating others. The idea of beating his teachers at football held great appeal. In the last minute of the game the score was tied and Dave held the ball for one final play. Jim stood near him, his arms outstretched, his pleading eyes saying the words he was unable to speak: 'Throw it to me, Dave, throw it to me.'

"For a moment Dave's struggle was reflected in his face: his desire to win vs. those imploring eyes. Then Dave threw the ball—to Jim. Jim clasped it joyfully to his chest and dashed for the end zone.

"As he crossed the goal, the students picked him up and carried him on their shoulders. At the same moment, the teachers picked up Dave and carried him on their shoulders. No one mentioned the fact that Jim had run to the wrong goal."

Sadly, sports stories such as this are rare indeed in the cutthroat competitive world of modern America. The wonderful old maxim, "It's not whether you win or lose, but how you play the game," is lost in the desperation to win, to have it all. President Richard Nixon's own philosophy was reflected in the lines he attributed to his high school coach: "A good loser is still a loser." Although many achievers in today's competitive American society adhere to Nixon's philosophy, many others are sensitive to its potentially destructive message. In his monumental book *Sports in America,* the celebrated author James Michener refused to include a chapter on the often-touted "character-building" aspect of sports. In fact, he said, sports had saved him from a life of crime as a young boy, provided his only means to a college education through a basketball scholarship, and literally saved his life when he had a heart attack; however, he had learned from experience that many of the great athletes were utter failures in later life, and many of the world's great leaders had been failures as young athletes.

Nothing exposes this dark side of sports so much as the way homosexuals in sports have been dealt with over the years. Ignoring

Greek athletes in training for the ancient Olympic games. The ancient Olympics were open only to male competitors; women were forbidden not only to compete but even to watch.

17

As a decathlete in the 1968 Olympic Games, Dr. Tom Waddell demonstrated himself to be a world-class athlete, but as the founder of the Gay Games he rejected one common notion of athletic competition by encouraging its participants to compete against themselves, not one another.

the Judeo-Christian teachings about the meek inheriting the earth, in too many cases athletes have turned on the weak, brutally shunning all those who were in any way "different," especially the effeminate boys, masculine girls, sissies, tomboys, queers. (Of course, it should be remembered that interest or disinterest in sports is not in and of itself any indication of sexual orientation. Neither are artistic inclinations.)

In nearly every homosexual's biography a similar experience of wanting desperately to be accepted as a child but never quite making the team is related. The late gay publisher David Goodstein told David Kopay something he said he had never been able to tell anyone. He said he had always despised jocks because of a humiliating childhood experience that had left him scarred for life. Goodstein by this time had retired after a brilliant career as an investment banker and had founded the highly regarded national gay journal, the *Advocate*. He was a success by anybody's measure, but he could never forget a certain childhood experience: a group of bigger, older boys, athletes, chased him, held him down, and urinated on him, cursing him and calling him a sissy, a faggot.

Kopay had denied his own homosexuality for many years, but he had never indulged in such violent actions against his own kind. However, many others did; more often than not such behavior was yet another form of denial, another mask behind which to hide one's own homosexuality. In his book *Queer in America,* Michelangelo Signorile tells about joining in when the other fellows chased down the sissies and faggots and threw basketballs at them. He tells the story with deep remorse because by the time of his writing, he had himself been hit with many a figurative basketball thrown by others because of his own homosexuality.

The novelist Andrew Holleran has written about his own childhood struggle with masculinity in general terms: "You knew what it was when you were small—it was certain boys, who played in groups, tortured cats, threw stones at birds, teased little girls by throwing lizards at them. (I could give you names.) They scared you. They seemed to have a mean edge. They were dangerous. They tied a rope to the high platform diving board, and knotted this rope, and swung far out over the water—a nine-year-old's version of bungee jumping. Boys, real boys, were not afraid, it seemed, early on in life—of deep water, high jumps, or other boys. They wandered in packs. Like dogs. They joined Cub Scouts, then Boy Scouts. They came to your house to settle grudges and made you go out and fight. They played baseball. At baseball practice, you prayed the ball would not be hit in your direction; when it was, you held your glove up the way a waiter hoists a tray—a flat surface, the ball, when it did hit, merely bounced off of it. What was preventing you from closing your mitt on the ball? Why does the sight of boys playing baseball depress you even now?"

Holleran's questions are not so easily answered, especially by young women whose first encounters with sports were so very different from the boys' kind he describes. In general, until the last few decades, little boys were considered weak and different if they did not play sports, while little girls were looked on with similar disdain if they wanted to play. A middle-aged woman wrote to *Ms.* magazine in 1975 that "in high school, I ran like the wind, but there was no track for females."

With the enactment of the federal legislation known as Title IX, which prohibits discrimination against women in schools and colleges receiving federal aid, the gross imbalance in men's and women's athletics began to change. But for many women it has been a classic case of two steps forward, three steps back. The more American sports are opened up to women, the more widespread are the accusations that discredit these pioneers by alleging that all women athletes are lesbians. The more popular men's and now women's sports become, the more the coaches and corporate owners dig in their heels and swear that there are no homosexuals playing in college and professional sports today.

In 1975, reporter Lynn Rosellini could not find a single athlete on any level of American sports who would talk openly about his or her homosexuality until David Kopay volunteered for her pioneering series, *Gays in Sports,* in the *Washington Star.* Eighteen years later reporter Barry Meisel wrote a series on the same subject for the *New York Daily News,* which was widely syndicated and published in newspapers throughout America. Much to his amazement, Meisel found that attitudes in the sports establishment about homosexuals remained rigid. Meisel encountered a wall of silence when he tried to interview coaches and owners; they either refused outright to talk with him, or assured him they had no problem with homosexuality because no homosexuals were playing on their teams.

What it comes down to is that after the sexual revolution of the 1960s and all the societal changes that accompanied it, the world of sports has changed very little in its outlook toward homosexuals. Only one human being—tennis champion Martina Navratilova, arguably the greatest woman player in the history of the sport—in the entire world of big-time amateur and professional sports in America is openly gay.

But, as often happens among those who are shunned by the larger society, homosexuals have taken matters into their own hands. They began to organize teams and clubs on a small local scale at first. If the straight teams were not comfortable places for sissies and tomboys, then gays and lesbians would organize leagues of their own.

When Dr. Tom Waddell began planning a separate Olympic games for gays and lesbians in 1980, he found thousands of people out there ready and waiting for such an event. A champion athlete himself, Waddell had been a member of the U.S. decathlon team at the 1968 Olympics in Mexico City. While it saw nothing wrong with older Americans using the name for a Senior Olympics, or with the Kennedys using it for the Special Olympics for the physically or mentally impaired, the U.S. Olympic Committee (USOC) saw red when a gay man tried to use the name for a sporting event for homosexuals. The USOC spent millions of dollars fighting the Gay Olympics, all the way to the U.S. Supreme Court, where the homosexuals lost.

Undeterred, Waddell's Gay Olympics became the Gay Games and went ahead, opening to a few spirited thousands in San Francisco in 1982. Held every four years, like the original olympiad, the Gay Games have steadily grown ever since—the first two were in San Francisco, the third in Vancouver, British Columbia. Gay Games IV, the most successful yet, was held in New York City in June 1994 and attracted more than 500,000 people to more than 30 different events. It is estimated that the event brought in more than $100 million to New York businesses. (Amsterdam, the Netherlands, is scheduled to be the host city for the 1998 Gay Games.) Figures such as this speak a language all Americans can understand and appreciate.

Maybe it is only fitting that changes in attitudes about homosexuals in sports and in America will come, finally, not out of any greater

*A runner breaks the tape at Gay Games III in Vancouver in 1990.
As youngsters, many gay men were driven from athletics by the prevailing macho stereotypes and a competitive ethic that left little place for the
less athletically gifted. As adults, many have rediscovered the joys of
participating in athletics in such forums as the Gay Games and others.*

tolerance on the part of the larger society, but because homosexuals themselves took charge and made a success of what once seemed a silly idea, having a gay Olympics.

Many gay and lesbian athletes say that the Gay Games have changed their lives. After winning a gold medal in the 1984 Olympics, Bruce Hayes put competitive swimming behind him because he felt that his athletic ability was incompatible with his homosexuality. In 1990 he went to Vancouver to compete in the third Gay Games. "I think of the Gay Games as having changed my life," Hayes said. "In 1990, I was just getting back into swimming. I had gotten out of swimming because it was scary to think of being an out gay man. But when I heard of the Gay Games, I realized there was finally an event that actually melded the two aspects of my life."

Tom Waddell dreamed of a new philosophy for sports when he began organizing the Gay Games. Nobody—including straight people—would be excluded. Waddell said that "doing one's personal best should be the paramount goal in any athletic endeavor."

Bruce Hayes says, "Winning a gold medal at the 1984 Olympics was everything I always hoped it would be, but participating in the Gay Games was, in many ways, the most satisfying and gratifying experience of my athletic career."

Gay and lesbian athletes have now taken charge of their own athletic challenges. They are fighting homophobia in sports by defying age-old stereotypes. In doing that, they are setting an example for a new generation of young athletes to follow. They are also showing the larger society how truly wholesome sports can be. By their example, they could help to change society's attitudes about homosexuals and about sports. The official slogan for Gay Games IV was Games Can Change the World. After a long and shameful history of oppression, there may be a happy ending, after all, to the story of gays and lesbians in sports.

2

Women, Sports, and the L Word

In books such as The Stronger Women Get, the More Men Love Football, *former collegiate and professional basketball player Mariah Burton Nelson has examined the issue of gender and athletics. Burton Nelson believes that "sport, with its physical empowerment and lesbian potential, is an inherently feminist act."*

IN THE MIDDLE OF the 1981–82 college basketball season, Pam Parsons, coach of the women's team at the University of South Carolina, had a record any coach would be proud of. Her team was undefeated and ranked number two in the nation. Abruptly, on New Year's Eve, Parsons resigned amid a flurry of rumors and accusations. *Sports Illustrated* reported allegations that the famous coach was involved in a love affair with one of her players, Tina Buck.

In a desperate attempt to regain their reputations, Parsons and Buck denied their relationship. They sued *Sports Illustrated* for libel, demanding $75 million in damages. To their horror, the two women found themselves in a situation much like the one experienced by the brilliant Anglo-Irish writer Oscar Wilde a hundred years earlier. Publicly branded a "somdomite" by John Douglas, the poor-spelling eighth Marquess of Queensberry and the noble father of his young male companion, Wilde had sued for slander and lost, only to then be tried himself under England's criminal statutes forbidding sexual relations between men, convicted, and sentenced to prison. Like Wilde, Parsons and Buck brought suit to restore their reputations, only to be subsequently tried themselves—in their case, for perjury regarding allegedly false sworn testimony that they gave regarding the nature of their relationship to one another. They were convicted and sentenced to four months in jail.

Ironically, these women suffered only because they were doing what they thought society and women's sports expected, even demanded, of them: keeping their sexual orientation hidden in a closet. The scandalous conclusion to the case of Parsons and Buck makes the difficult position of the lesbian in women's sports painfully clear: if you tell the truth, you will not make the team; if you lie, you might get convicted of perjury. Though it might be argued that Parsons and Buck brought about their own imprisonment, if not all their troubles, by bringing the libel suit, the two, like Wilde before them, surely felt that they had no choice in the matter: once they had been publicly branded as homosexuals, their careers, if not their lives, had been irreparably damaged, if not destroyed. The lawsuits were a way of trying to push the closet door shut again, to regain the privacy that others had surrendered for them.

"Women's athletics is, in fact, held hostage to fear of the 'L word,'" says Pat Griffin, an associate professor of physical education at the University of Massachussetts at Amherst. Although Griffin herself lives openly as a lesbian, she has witnessed the immense harm that can be done by rumors and gossip about homosexuality in connection with a player or a coach.

In 1988 a survey called *The Wilson Report: Moms, Dads, Daughters and Sports* examined the attitudes on gender and athletics of a selected group of girls between the ages of 7 and 18. Thirty-six percent felt that boys made fun of girls who played sports. For a confused young teenager, the taunts of "tomboy" can be a terrifying experience at an age when fitting in is so important. And as a young girl grows older, the tomboy image is likely to carry with it the "taint" of lesbianism— especially in college and professional women's sports.

In 1975, Mariah Burton Nelson was a player on the women's basketball team at Stanford University in California. Her teammates knew that she was a lesbian and there were no problems, perhaps because Stanford has long been an educational institution that prides itself on tolerance and a progressive political attitude. (As the experience of Buck and Parsons shows, acceptance of lesbian athletes is by no means universal on college campuses.) However, later, as a member of the San Francisco Pioneers, a team in a short-lived professional league, Nelson was placed on waivers for appearing in a gay pride parade. Being fired from the Women's Pro Basketball League for being a lesbian, said Nelson, is "akin to being fired from the National Basketball Association for being black."

In 1972 the congressional act known as Title IX became law, prohibiting discrimination against women in schools and colleges that received federal aid. In hundreds of places, there had been no sports programs for women at all, and where there were, the women's programs were universally inferior. Except for a tiny number of major universities, no schools offered athletic scholarships to women.

Largely because of Title IX, women athletes, especially on the collegiate level, have made phenomenal gains in the last two decades. Where there were no scholarships for women at all two decades ago, there are now more than 12,000 scholarships available in 22 different college sports. Several women's athletic events, most notably the collegiate basketball championship tournament, are now nationally televised.

The new female athletes are pioneers in all kinds of ways. First and foremost, they are fighting stereotypes—especially the one that holds that just as no male athlete (those epitomes of masculinity) could possibly be gay, all female athletes must be lesbian. Neither, of course, is true. What is equally true, of course, as a number of athletes have demonstrated, is that those athletes who are gay or lesbian are not necessarily lesser athletes or lesser men or women than their fellow competitors.

What women involved in the new college and professional women's athletic programs have discovered is that the arguments over gender and sexuality may be concerned as much with economics as they are with homophobia. Don Sabo, who has been a close observer of American sports for many years and has published several books on sports psychology, says, "Many so-called gay issues are really sex-equity issues. Homophobia doesn't pertain to genitals but to jobs. It doesn't pertain to preference as much as it does to opportunity. Homophobia in sports perpetuates male dominance and the male monopoly of existing resources."

That is, the labeling of women athletes as lesbians and women's athletics as a bastion of homosexuality helps keep women's athletics in a place of secondary status—in terms of money, media coverage, and fan interest—as compared with men's athletics. It also serves, of course, to reinforce traditional (that is, essentially male-defined) notions of femininity, which hold competitiveness (beginning on the athletic fields but extending into all aspects of society, especially the job marketplace) to be "unbecoming" in a woman, unladylike, unattractive. If, as has often been argued to justify Americans' obsession with sports, athletics is a training ground on which to instill those virtues necessary to compete and excel in American society, what does it say about that society's notions of the rightful place of women when it holds that such training is not as necessary for them as it is for young men?

The great Olympic heptathlete Jackie Joyner-Kersee is quoted by Mariah Burton Nelson in *Are We Winning Yet? How Women Are Changing Sports and Sports Are Changing Women:* "It used to be, you couldn't play basketball or any sport without, 'Oh, she's a lesbian.' Now it's a little better. But it's something they do to keep you from playing sports. That's all it's about."

Why this is true is a complex and fascinating question. While the roles of women in society are changing dramatically, some of these changes are coming at a remarkably slow pace. Nelson believes that

*Pam Parsons was an extremely successful women's basketball coach
at the collegiate level before publicity regarding her love affair with one
of her players wound up costing her her position at the University of
South Carolina. Though it can be argued that any sexual relationship
between a player and a coach, be it a heterosexual or a homosexual
one, is an impermissible breach of the proper relationship between
a team and its coach, it's doubtful if the Parsons affair would have
been deemed so newsworthy by the media if the participants were
not both women.*

"homophobia in sports serves as a way to control women, both gay and straight, and it reflects a gross misunderstanding of who women are as physical and sexual beings." Pat Griffin says that, "Women's athletics is, in fact, held hostage to fear of the 'L word.' As long as women's athletics continues to deny that there are lesbians in sport . . . we will never control our sporting lives and will be forced to waste energy defending a counterfeit heterosexual-only image that we all know is a lie." Although Nelson insists in her book that the majority of women athletes are heterosexual, she says the figure is nowhere near the 90 percent that is often cited for the society at large.

One important reason that such thinking persists is that while women have made great strides as players and even as coaches, the vast majority of women's teams are still coached by men, and virtually all of the college and professional associations women play in are dominated by men; some have only token female representation on their governing boards, and many have none.

Betty Jaynes, executive director of the Women's Basketball Coaches Association, has said, "We're losing women in coaching because they're afraid of being labeled lesbians. We've got to find a way to stop it." Pat Griffin showed by example that one way to stop it is to start being honest with yourself. Mariah Burton Nelson asked Griffin what happened when she started talking openly about being a lesbian. "Nothing happened," said Griffin. In fact, she says that the workshops she offers to combat homophobia in sports are always "filled beyond capacity. People are eager to break the long silence."

All changes that affect an entire culture naturally come slowly; when these changes regard sex and sex roles, they are often especially painful because no issue cuts closer to questions of personal identity and because many people hold to the old ways with a genuine religious fervor. In sports as in society in general, the major change is that people are now talking openly about subjects that everybody knew about but nobody talked about before, breaking a silence that led to a general denial and blatant hypocrisy regarding gays and lesbians. However, the hypocrisy in sports over homosexuality seems even more shocking as regards women than men. Perhaps it is because we are conditioned to think of women as more sensitive, more humane; perhaps, ironically, because they were not schooled in the same crucible of competition as were men. We expect men to be full of bluff and bluster, all swagger and intimidation; we assume that women are more honest with themselves and the rest of the world. Women were not taught that winning is everything and to measure their self-worth in victory over another; they were taught (or so another stereotype has it) the importance of striving together and sharing—the original definition of "compete." Among many women, at least, how you play the game, not winning, is still the most important part of it.

And so it is dismaying to learn that the most rampant hypocrisy regarding homosexuality in sports exists in those two sports, golf and basketball, that were among the first to be open to women—and where lesbians have always been counted among the brightest and best players.

In Mariah Nelson's book there is a shocking story told by a champion golfer on the professional women's tour, the Ladies Professional Golf Association (LPGA). She agreed to talk about her homosexuality only if Nelson would change her name and alter facts of her life so nobody would be able to identify her. A conservative Republican, she is critical of lesbian activists, including Martina Navratilova. She accepts the widely quoted notion that the LPGA's corporate sponsors might withdraw their support if the true number of lesbian players was ever known. In fact, she does everything she can to counter this lesbian image—putting on makeup for a golf match as if she is going to an old-time debutante ball.

Nelson opens her chapter on lesbians in sports, titled "A Silence So Loud It Screams," by following this woman, whom she calls "Angie," onto the golf course. One thing that particularly irritates Angie are the lesbians who show up in the crowds and then spend their time talking about how cute the players are rather than how well they play the game. Angie travels with her lover-companion, "Suzanne," one of whose jobs is to shoo away lesbian fans if they become too obvious. One day at an unspecified golf tournament, there were two in the "diesel dyke and mud wrestler" category, so Suzanne did her job. The women politely left, but not without telling Suzanne they had driven 7 hours just to see

Mariah Burton Nelson (dribbling, with bandages on both knees) on the hardwood. "Basketball doesn't threaten my femininity," she once told a television reporter while she was a member of the San Francisco Pioneers of the Women's Pro Basketball League. "But it does seem to threaten some men."

Angie play and that one of them had just finished a 12-hour shift on her job. To her credit, Angie did have the grace to feel a little bad afterward: "I didn't even acknowledge them, or thank them for coming as I would a beer-bellied, beer-drinking man."

Many insiders joke that they know what the *L* really stands for in the LPGA. According to journalist Susan Reed, writing in the June 1994 issue of *Out* magazine, "players estimate that 30 to 40 percent of the women playing professional golf are lesbians." And the LPGA itself was apparently so worried about its lesbian image that a beautician and fashion consultant were hired to travel to 20 LPGA tournaments every year and help with makeup and clothes and all the little things that make women look more "feminine."

Women golfers have come a long way, and they are not about to relinquish what they have gained. Prize money is now 300 percent higher than it was 10 years ago. While corporate sponsorship is stronger than ever, everybody knows that sponsorship can disappear in a minute. Avon cosmetics threatened to withdraw its support of women's tennis after just one player, Billie Jean King, admitted that she had had a lesbian love affair. Among the members of the LPGA, fear of the economic consequences of disclosure remains great. "Because it would be suicide," a lesbian member of the tour told *Out* magazine in June 1994 in response to being asked why she did not come out. "Because you'd get cut off from every endorsement opportunity possible. Because there's money and careers at stake." This same golfer spoke about a meeting she attended shortly after joining the women's tour. "There was a mandatory players' meeting once," she told *Out*. "One of the top players, [a lesbian], led the meeting. She told us, 'Ladies, we do not care what goes on inside your bedroom. But keep it there.' The message was loud and clear: for the golf tour to succeed, we need to rid ourselves of the lesbian stigma."

The hypocrisy involved in the LPGA's lesbian denial is all the greater because the organization was founded by one of the greatest golfers of all time, Babe Didrikson Zaharias, an Olympic athlete who was known to be an active lesbian—though she married a man—by nearly all those who ever worked with her. One can understand the very practical reasons why the women in the LPGA are running scared, but one also wonders if everybody would not be better off—at least from a moral and mental health standpoint—if the women golfers were a little more true to their history, true to themselves. Nelson says, "Any form of dishonesty upsets me, and I think the LPGA is deliberately trying to fool people by trying to portray this traditional feminine image." Maybe the image is traditionally feminine, but it most assuredly is not traditionally women's golf.

Basketball is another American invention that has been exported to nearly every country in the world. The game was created in 1891 by James Naismith of the Young Men's Christian Association (YMCA) in Springfield, Massachusetts, at the suggestion of Dr. Luther H. Gulick. It filled a need at the YMCA for a game to be played indoors between football and baseball seasons. Although it was promoted by the YMCA, women were encouraged to play the game from the beginning, and in 1899 a separate set of rules was drawn up for them. (The original rules made women's basketball a dramatically different game from the men's version; today, with some minor exceptions—among them a slightly smaller ball—women hoopsters play by the same rules as men.) By 1950 supporters of basketball were declaring it the national game of the United States, claiming that more people played the sport than any other team sport and that basketball had more paid spectators than football and baseball combined. In the more than four decades since, the sport's popularity has continued to expand, both in the United States and abroad, to the point that by the turn of the century it is expected to displace soccer as the world's most popular sport.

As a direct result of Title IX, women's basketball got a new life on college campuses throughout America. With a new source of players, professional women's basketball briefly took on a new life, although it has never approached the success of the collegiate version of the game or of male professional leagues.

But with the new successes, the old "taint" of lesbianism in women's sports became an even greater problem. Like Pat Griffin, Mariah Burton Nelson experienced no homophobia when her teammates on the

The cover of Burton Nelson's first book. Nelson is one of many who believe that homophobia serves to perpetuate dominant, largely male-created stereotypes about gender roles. According to Lucille Kyvallos, the former women's basketball coach at Queens College, "Men see sport as a way to express masculinity and competitiveness. If you are a confident woman athlete, men are threatened. If you are a confident lesbian athlete, they are even more threatened."

ARE WE WINNING YET?
How Women Are Changing Sports and Sports are Changing Women

MARIAH BURTON NELSON

Stanford women's basketball team learned that she was a lesbian. Others have not been so lucky.

In her series about lesbians and gays in sports for the *Detroit Free Press*, Michelle Kaufman included a sequence of horror stories of lives ruined by mere gossip and rumors of homosexuality. One important woman in the sport, who conducts a popular basketball camp for young women, is supposed to have a list of college coaches who are lesbians, which is used to steer potential recruits away from those colleges. Apparently nobody knows for sure whether such a list exists, but, as Pat Griffin explains, "whether the list exists or not doesn't matter. The threat of the list is enough to keep women in their place. And what people don't realize is that a female athlete has a greater chance of being seduced and harassed by a heterosexual male than a lesbian."

One college player told Kaufman that the reason she went to the University of Iowa was because the women's coach was a married

Pat Griffin is an associate professor of physical education at the University of Massachusetts. Griffin believes that women's athletics would benefit from a more truthful approach to the issue of lesbianism.

woman. "Coaches and players were telling me not to go to certain schools because the coach was gay. It scares you at 17. That's unfair and it makes me sound like a terrible person, but I'm being honest." Yet another college player said she ignored all the negative gossip she heard about another coach because the only things that mattered to her were the coach's "stats" and the school's academic record. "Who the coach slept with was not my concern, but my mother cared. One of the first questions she asked was whether anyone on the team was gay. I'm her baby and she was worried."

Another mother in Texas wreaked havoc in 1993 when she yanked her daughter home from tryouts for the University of Texas Lady Longhorns' team because of all the talk about lesbians there. Louise Swoopes told the *Austin American-Statesman* that her daughter, Sheryl Swoopes, had been subjected to sexual advances by two lesbian members of the Texas team. Swoopes, a member of the Texas Tech national champions, had been voted most valuable player in the NCAA tournament. She had transferred to the University of Texas and was already living on the Austin campus when she abruptly quit and went home.

To her credit, Jody Conradt, the coach of the Lady Longhorns, refused to be intimidated by the accusations. Conradt said she knew nothing of the incidents Swoopes's mother described, but she said it was no problem for her or the team if there were active lesbian members. The winningest coach in women's basketball, Conradt has an overall record of 620 wins, including one national championship, and 153 losses. Conradt said the university had a policy not to discriminate against anyone because of sexual orientation.

"The best team I ever had had diversity," Conradt said. "When our society learns to embrace diversity, we'll be a lot better society."

One of the most widely publicized antilesbian incidents involved Rene Portland, coach of the women's basketball team at Pennsylvania State University. Until two years ago, Portland had four team rules: no drinking, no drugs, no jeans on the road, no lesbians. She told recruits that she would not tolerate homosexuality and that the scholarship of any player she learned was lesbian would be revoked.

When the *Philadelphia Inquirer* reported this story, Portland refused to deny it, saying only that she had "training rules." Mariah Burton Nelson asks, "Can you imagine if Rene Portland had said she doesn't allow Jews or blacks on her team? She would have been fired." Portland was not fired, but she was required by the university to attend a homosexual awareness workshop. Eventually, she did revoke her antilesbian policy. An important reason why the media pressed Portland so hard on this issue was because a number of sportswriters are themselves gay, according to Judy Van Handle, an editor at the *Boston Globe* who is herself openly lesbian.

Although this may be true, and while the press in general enjoys a reputation for liberality and enlightenment, most reporters would agree that the sports pages are the last bastions of male dominance on most newspapers and are still a home for homophobia. According to Leroy F. Aarons, a former editor at the *Washington Post* and vice president for news of the Oakland *Tribune,* "There are probably more homophobic comments made in sports sections than in other sections. Gays and lesbians may tend to gravitate to living sections because colleagues there are more tolerant. People go where they feel comfortable." Aarons is the founder of the National Lesbian and Gay Journalists Association, a group made up largely of homosexuals who work in the straight media. The group includes some of the most outstanding journalists in the country, who are now able to work in the media without feeling the need to hide their homosexuality (although there are doubtless as many more who remain closeted, still fearful of repercussions if others knew they were gay). Whatever the liberal reputation of the media, the newsroom was long a bastion of male supremacy until women reporters and editors began asserting their rights in the 1970s and 1980s; now, homosexual reporters and editors are making their voices heard.

The media exercise a subtle but vast and pervasive influence on American society. It is impossible to measure just how much these recent changes inside the newsrooms will eventually affect the society in general. One place where you no longer will hear fag jokes is the sports department of the *Portland Oregonian,* where reporter Abby

Haight is open about being a lesbian. She scoffs at the old stereotypes that hold that "there are no gay male athletes, all women athletes are dykes." She refutes this by her own example: "That's like saying all gay journalists work in the living sections. Well, I'm gay, and I write sports."

The changes in attitudes about homosexuals in sports are painfully slow in coming. They affect our most deeply held prejudices and fears. But it is heartening to hear about the changes in places as far-flung as Portland, Austin, and College Station, Pennsylvania (home to Penn State). They offer hope that change may also come to the rest of America.

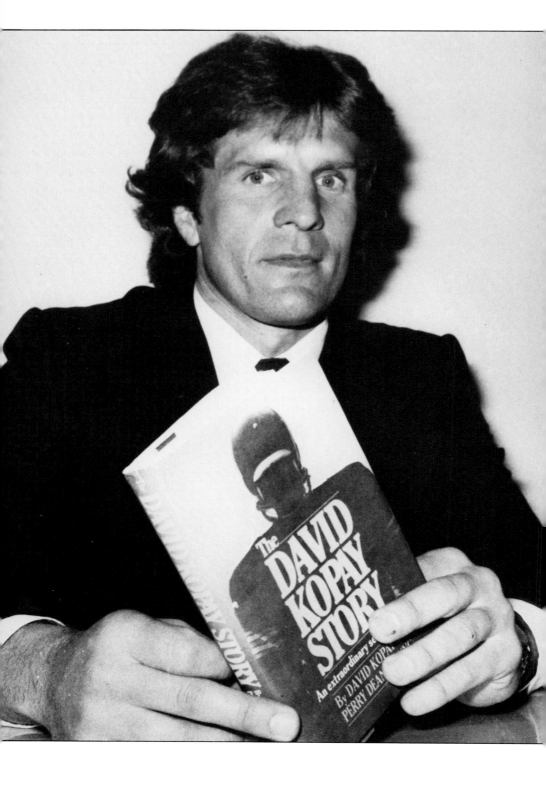

3

Football

IF AMERICA WERE AN isolated island somewhere, visiting anthropologists might well seize on football as the sport that best defined and explained the larger culture. Modern American football is the product of a male-dominated society, with brute force the main weapon in a game of territory.

Like their European ancestors, Americans have always been fond of kicking around a ball. In the rough pioneer days it was literally a pigskin, a pig's bladder blown up and tied in a knot. Emigrants to America had shared in the traditions that created European "football"—which Americans call soccer—but the older version is like a ballet compared to the rough and even dangerous sport that developed in the United States. A new form of English football—rugby—was founded at the British school of the same name in 1823, when William Webb Ellis, "with a fine disregard of the rules of football, as played in his time, first took the ball in his arms and ran with it."

In late 1975 Dave Kopay's revelation that he was gay caused a sensation in the sports world. Even more so than today, prevailing stereotypes held male homosexuality to be incompatible with athleticism, particularly in the world of professional football, which was widely regarded as the most quintessentially masculine of American sports.

Young Americans were supposed to be playing the game as it was played at Eton and Rugby, but the American game quickly took on a far more violent character than its European progenitor. The "bloody Monday" games at Yale and Harvard became so violent they were banned in 1858 and 1860.

American football players continued blithely on, ignoring the polite European rules of rugby and soccer and developing a rough game of their own. It is the only American sport that has never been successfully exported. Anthropologist William Arens has written, "A love of football is one of the few interests we share with few outside our borders, but with almost everyone within them." More Americans watch the National Football League (NFL)'s annual Super Bowl on television than have ever witnessed any other single event in history.

Anthropologist Konrad Lorenz surely had American football in mind in his book *On Aggression* when he observed: "The main function of sport today lies in the cathartic discharge of the aggressive urge." Vince Lombardi, one of the most famous and successful coaches in the history of the sport, offered a similar opinion: "I think the nature of man is to be aggressive and football is a violent game. But I think the very violence is one of the great things about the game because a man has to learn control. He is going to go in and knock somebody's block off, and yet he must keep a rein on it." Football players themselves frequently compare football to combat in warfare, although they surely would not make the comparison if they had ever experienced the very real terrors and humiliations of actual combat. Wayne Walker, a former linebacker with the Detroit Lions, said, "Anybody who says this game is beastly, brutal and nasty, he's right." According to Larry Wilson, who was a Hall of Fame-caliber safety with the St. Louis Cardinals in the 1960s and is now an executive with the club (now located in Phoenix), "This is one way for people to release their aggressions. I see them coming out of the stands, they are wringing wet with sweat, they are mad, they have played a football game and they look as beat up as the football players on the field." Said John Niland, formerly a tackle with the Dallas Cowboys: "Let's face it, most of the people in our society enjoy watching one guy knock down another one."

The uniform and protective equipment developed for the sport serve to exaggerate the masculine ideal of broad shoulders, narrow waist, slim legs. Where, then, do homosexuals belong in this sport at the extreme edge of what Americans believe a man should be?

More than one observer of the American scene has said that football is possibly a homoerotic exercise for players and fans alike. As *Time* magazine reported in its November 13, 1978, issue, "A quarterback receives the ball from between the center's legs. After a successful play,

The publication of The David Kopay Story *occurred simultaneously with singer Anita Bryant's well-publicized homophobic remarks and activities. Kopay's book spent several weeks on the best-seller list; Bryant lost her position as a commercial spokesperson for orange juice and other products.*

teammates sometimes hug or slap each other on the bottom. The possible homosexual implications of these and other football rituals have long been noted by professional and amateur behaviorists alike. But none has studied the subject more closely than Alan Dundes, an anthropologist at the University of California in Berkeley."

In an article published in *Western Folklore,* Dundes observed that the "unequivocal sexual symbolism of the game" makes it clear that football is a homosexual ceremony. *Time* described Dundes's findings as showing that football is "a sanctioned form of theater where players and fans can safely discharge their homoerotic impulses." Dundes called it "a healthy outlet for male-to-male affection."

Reaction to Dundes's study was swift and predictable. University of California football coach Roger Theder called it "the most ridiculous thing I have ever heard." One of his freshman players said, "I was so angry, I just wanted to get my hands on the guy—I mean on his neck."

Today NFL team owners and coaches would all insist (as do the leaders of the military as regards gays in the military) that homosexuals do not belong in their league and that there are none playing in the National Football League today.

Thanks to the example of David Kopay, we now know that the truth is somewhat more complicated. In fact, we know about more homosexuals in professional football than in any other sport. Where better to hide one's own homosexuality than in the most masculine of sports, where homosexuals are supposed to be nonexistent? According to prevailing stereotypes of masculinity, the very fact that one is a football player would be proof against homosexuality.

That morning in December 1975, as he picked up a copy of the *Washington Star* and headed into a favorite breakfast place on Capitol Hill, David Kopay appeared to have everything going for him. He was six feet, 240 pounds of solid muscle. He moved with the self-assured agility of the successful athlete. His chiseled good looks, deep California tan, and long blond hair had just gotten him an invitation to appear as a centerfold in *Playgirl* magazine.

He would be the first to admit that as a player he had never been a superstar, but he had lasted 10 years (as a running back and special teams player) in the NFL, something only a tiny percentage of men in his sport ever do, and had always been a favorite of coaches and teammates for his grit, determination, and heart. Yet now that his football career was over, he had been unable to get any kind of sports-related job.

Moreover, Kopay was currently dealing with intense inner confusion about his sexual identity, about what he appeared to be and who he really was. As he sat down to breakfast that winter morning in 1975, he opened the *Star* to the sports pages and was stunned by the headline he read over the first article in Lynn Rosellini's series: HOMOSEXUALS IN SPORTS.

It was a subject Kopay was painfully aware of, but never before had he heard it discussed in public, much less seen it examined in print. As he read on, he came to an anonymous interview with one of the best players in the NFL. Rosellini described the player's big, scarred hands and let him tell about his agonizing double life as a star pro football player and secret homosexual. The player held up honesty and openness as the ideal he wanted in his life, he said, but he could never go public about being gay because he would be fired as a player, and it would cause needless suffering to his family and possibly irreparable damage to the business he had worked so hard to build. But, he asked wistfully, is America really about lying to fit the "Mom and apple pie" stereotypes, or is it about being honest?

Kopay knew instantly that the unnamed player was his old friend, his original love, Jerry Smith, the all-pro tight end with the Washington Redskins. For a second Kopay felt slightly betrayed, but he experienced intense, overwhelming elation that the word was finally out, that even the newspapers were now describing homosexuals in sports; nobody could ever again say it was not true. He and Smith had talked long hours about their predicament. They had agreed somebody had to write a book about it and felt they might write it together. In fact, the two men had a great deal in common. They were both blonds, both six feet tall, weighed 240 pounds each, wore the same size clothes, and were only one year apart in age. Both had grown up in California, been reared in working-class, devout Catholic families. The competitive athlete in Kopay could not stand it that Smith had finished first, made it to their shared goal of talking about homosexuality. He kept trying to reach Smith, but his old friend was never in and never managed to return his calls—and would not for another year.

By this time, with, he believed, rumors about his homosexuality keeping him from getting any kind of coaching job even though he had gone through dozens of interviews, Kopay felt he had nothing left to lose. "At least I can do that," he said; at least he could be honest about his own name.

He called Rosellini; she interviewed him that day and the story ran in the next day's *Star*. As one gay newspaper columnist observed, "Just by standing still and saying who he was, Kopay had reaped a whirlwind." Rosellini had spent hours researching all of the major sports; she had published 20 different articles over five days. But the only one anybody would remember was the article about football and Kopay, in which Rosellini had mentioned that three NFL quarterbacks were known to be gay and that several players on the Redskins were also gay.

After Rosellini's article about him was published, Kopay became an overnight celebrity, interviewed by Phil Donahue, David Susskind, Geraldo Rivera, and by nearly all the other hosts of major television talk shows. Some gay leaders were resentful at having a jock as a gay spokesman because "nobody ever called him sissy." But most of the gay political leaders were thrilled to have Kopay as a new spokesman and role model. The gay writer Merle Miller said, "This is history; he has killed a stereotype overnight."

The public reaction to Kopay's disclosure was almost all positive. The same could not be said of that of his family. His parents were so humiliated that they sold their house in Los Angeles and moved to Sacramento; his older brother complained that David had cost him the head coaching job at the University of Oregon.

Meanwhile, Kopay signed a book contract. The book's creation was a painful process for him. I became his collaborator on the book, and I put him through a grueling set of interviews, forcing him to face up to all the questions he had spent a lifetime dodging. One friend said that Kopay went through "five years of therapy in six months." But the truth was, Kopay had been thrust into the role of expert on homosexuality when he had just begun to learn about it himself. He endured my interrogations because he understood that the book was a more serious and lasting contribution than all the talk-show appearances, and by telling about his own life and experiences he might help to dispel some myths and make some space where other homosexual athletes could live without fear of being "found out."

When the weather was nice, we would go outside to a little park at the edge of Georgetown in Washington. We would sit across from each other at a picnic table, with me asking the questions, Kopay doing his best to answer them. One day, after I kept trying to get more details about an especially trying moment in his life, Kopay laid his head down and cried. "When will it not be so emotional?" he asked. "I can't answer that," I said, "but that's what makes this an important story."

Kopay had been scheduled to play in the annual varsity-alumni game in May of 1976 at the University of Washington, where he had been cocaptain of the 1964 Pacific Eight championship team that went to the Rose Bowl. He was nervous about facing his old teammates, his old fans; he was even more nervous about seeing his family. This trip back in time was the source of the last chapters in our book, *The David Kopay Story: An Extraordinary Self-Revelation.* The varsity-alumni game that spring was the first game played in Seattle's new King Dome. Kopay's old friends and teammates welcomed him back as they always had; they even elected him captain of the alumni team. Behind the scenes, officials were worried about what might happen; instead of having the coin toss on the field, they had it on the sidelines so Kopay would not be such an obvious target if some nut decided to take a shot at him. This, after all, was what had happened to the fictional young runner in Patricia Nell Warren's novel, *The Front Runner,* who overcomes the private and public hell involved with being the only openly gay athlete—only to get gunned down by an assassin at the Olympics. Warren had signed a copy of her book for Kopay, "For the real life front runner."

Kopay himself was nervous about how the crowd would react, but when his name was called and he ran onto the field, all he could hear was applause.

.

Tight end Jerry Smith was Kopay's teammate on the Washington Redskins and onetime lover. As a player, Smith was unusual for more than his sexuality. At the time, tight ends were usually valued more for their blocking than pass-catching ability. Comparatively slight compared to others who played his position, Smith used his speed and outstanding hands to make himself a threat as a downfield receiver and became a favorite target of Washington's Hall of Fame quarterback, Sonny Jurgensen.

It took time, but Kopay never gave up on his family, and they ended up being far closer than they had ever been before. *The David Kopay Story* was published in March 1977, the same day that singer and television commercial spokesperson Anita Bryant became a national symbol of homophobia by founding a group in Miami to fight that city's human rights ordinances, which included homosexuals among the groups protected under their provisions. Kopay visited nearly every major American city in the months that followed. Among the hundreds of speeches he gave were addresses to the national conventions of the American Bar Association and the American Association of Pediatricians. For many of these organizations, Kopay's discussions marked the first time they had held a public discussion of homosexuality. Most gratifying to Kopay, he received more than 30,000 letters from people who said reading his story had changed their lives. The sister of a famous National Hockey League player wrote that she now understood the agony of her brother's double life as a homosexual and a star athlete. Hundreds of young athletes wrote to say how much their own lonely struggles paralleled Kopay's and how grateful they were to him for telling the world they were not alone.

David Kopay and Jerry Smith were hardly the first or only homosexuals ever to play for the Redskins. A few years earlier, a promising young black player had joined the team. The coaches and owners discovered that he was homosexual the worst possible way: he was arrested for sexual activity in Lafayette Park, across from the White House. (The park had for many years been the only place in Washington where homosexuals could find each other.) After a second arrest, which, like the first, the Redskins managed to keep out of the newspapers, the player was released. He was never able to get another sports-related position, and he eventually changed his name in order to get a minimum-wage job as a public school janitor.

The general manager of the team, David Slattery, was secretly gay himself, although he never talked about it publicly until 1993. Of this early incident, Slattery now says that Vince Lombardi, the team's coach at the time, was not at all upset to learn he had a homosexual player; the only thing he worried about was the box office—what damage might be done if the public learned the Redskins had homosexual players.

When Dave Slattery talked with the *New York Daily News* about his homosexuality in 1993, he explained that for many years his workaholic lifestyle kept him from acknowledging his homosexuality even to himself. He was in his fifties before he ever acted on his natural impulses and had sex with another man. In spite of the fact that he was still working for the Redskins and in the closet about his sex life, Slattery was an active supporter of Kopay's public role, and he became a vital source of information behind the scenes for *The David Kopay Story*.

Kopay's three years with the Redskins had coincided with a traumatic time in his personal life. When he had first arrived at training camp, he had dressed in drab, conservative clothes, not wanting to draw attention to himself. Jerry Smith had quickly taken charge of that, and he soon had Kopay wearing flared trousers and bright colored shirts and going to a huge gay disco in Washington, so popular that it was often overrun with straights.

Several times the pair had ventured to Baltimore to a sleazy gay bar there; once, they had even gone to a gay bar in downtown Washington. Smith had dozens of aliases he used in these situations or when he would fly off to Cleveland or Miami or Acapulco. Needless to say, these two oversized athletes stood out in the dim gay bars. Smith would tell people he was a high school coach or a scout for some pro team. He actually seemed to enjoy living the double life at times. Going to the gay bars was not real to him—it was like putting on a costume and getting lost in a carnival. But Kopay was nothing but miserable with the double life. Acting was just not in his blood, and he could not live a lie.

Kopay and Smith were staying one night at the house of a Redskins official, who was also gay, when they finally went to bed together. For Kopay, the experience was overwhelming—love as he had never dared dream it could be. For Smith, it was just another toss in the hay. Kopay had had almost no homosexual experiences, but Smith had been very active for many years and soon would begin a sequence of long-term affairs with live-in lovers.

The two men never had sex again, but they remained close friends. They often shared the same room when the Redskins were on the road. One night, after a game and the revelry that followed, Smith drunkenly made his way down the hall and into the room and bed of another athlete, a stunningly beautiful man who could sing like an angel and was one of the team's most popular players. The next morning, the other player sought out Kopay and told him what his roommate had done. Although he said "it was really crazy," Kopay had the feeling this other player was not as judgmental as others would have been and actually sympathized with Smith. They sat together on the bus back to Washington, and the player told Kopay that he had had some emotional problems himself and had sought the help of a famous hypnotist-psychologist named William Jennings Bryan III. Weeks after the incident with Smith, Kopay tried to talk with this player about his own situation. But when he mentioned homosexuality, the other man abruptly ended the conversation and was never friendly to him again.

By this point, Kopay felt even more alone and confused, and he decided to go see the hypnotist his teammate had mentioned. This "hypnotist to the stars" had just been featured in *Esquire* magazine, and all kinds of prominent people said his treatment worked. Bryan assured Kopay he could cure his homosexuality; he had done it a thousand times. But the more the doctor tried to convince him he was not homosexual, the more Kopay realized that he was. Unfortunately, Bryan also talked Kopay into marrying a young stewardess that the player sometimes dated, made arrangements for the wedding in Las Vegas in the summer of 1973, and stood up as best man. Though the woman knew that Kopay was gay, she cared deeply for him. Nonetheless, the marriage was a mistake from the beginning, and Kopay bitterly regretted, for her sake, that this beautiful young woman had been used to "cure" his problem. They soon separated and were later divorced. With the failed marriage, Kopay knew for sure that there was no cure; homosexuality was a part of who he was and always had been.

In the years after Kopay left the Redskins and professional football, he stayed in touch with Jerry Smith. Even though his emotional life had been a shambles, Kopay had nonetheless loved living in the city of

Washington. And, every year come fall, wherever he was, he would start thinking about the leaves changing along the narrow streets of old Georgetown, which also meant, of course, that it was time for the start of football season. He and Smith would always get together for dinner and a night on the town when he got back to Washington. Smith, of course, was still playing and had to be careful, but that did not keep him from cruising the gay bars if he felt like it.

During the time we were writing the book, I despaired of not having access to Jerry Smith because I wanted to include him in the story and, if possible, to use his name and experiences as well. In fact, since we could not reach him, we had to call Jerry "Billy Stiles" in the book. We had also included a scene that may have embarrassed Smith. A mutual friend had told us that after Lynn Rosellini's story came out with the description of Smith's "scarred hands," Smith had worried about going into the office of his construction business. But when he did, his straight partner rushed over and grabbed his hand, saying, "We don't care if you do have scarred hands."

In other words, I felt at least partly responsible for the break between the two old friends. So, I invited them both to a party at my apartment. Much to my delight, Smith showed up with a fifth of tequila and a happy smile on his face. He grabbed Kopay in a genuine love hug, and the two sat down and caught up on each other's lives as if no book or anything else had ever come between them.

The David Kopay Story was on the *New York Times*'s best-seller list for nine weeks in 1977 (and was number 25 for the entire year); it was also honored as one of the best books of the year for young adults by the American Library Association. But despite the book's success, the world of sports remained closed to Kopay, and he tried a number of jobs before settling down at his uncle's discount floor-covering store, Linoleum City, in Hollywood. His uncle was a wry old fellow who always wore a beret. He had a large family of his own, but he brought Kopay into the business almost as if he were the prodigal son. A good part of the business involved selling to set designers at television and movie studios—and the uncle rightly figured that Kopay would be ideal for that job, since many of the designers were gay. He also told Kopay, "You know, I knew when you were a child that you were homosexual." Kopay laughed and said, "I wish to hell you had told me."

The ex–football star quickly adapted to the store's routine. He liked to get there early and have his coffee and read the sports pages before the place opened up. One morning in 1987 Kopay picked up the *Los Angeles Times,* got his coffee, unlocked the store, and sat down to read the ball scores. The headline hit him like a sledgehammer: ALL-PRO JERRY SMITH IS DYING OF AIDS.

It had not been that long since Kopay had talked with Smith. At that time, Smith was living with an older friend—not David Slattery, who was then living in Key West, but yet another closeted gay man who was still working in the Redskins' front office. This was the same friend whose house was where Kopay and Smith had had sex, still an important experience in Kopay's memory. Smith had said that his business was going through a down time, like the rest of the economy, and that he had had to sell his own house. He mentioned some minor ailments, but it did not sound like anything serious. Now, as he read the story, Kopay remembered Smith's talking about a bad cough that just would not go away, the same cough nearly all AIDS patients talk about having.

The *Los Angeles Times* story said Jerry was on his deathbed, in the last hideous throes of the disease. Recently a strapping 240-pounder, he was now an emaciated 98 pounds. It was also clear from the article that Jerry's mind had been affected; he had only rare moments of lucidity. In one of those moments, he had asked that a trusted old reporter for the *Washington Post* be called in to write his story, one who could be relied upon to write that he was dying of AIDS without ever mentioning that he was homosexual.

This was a final act that left Jerry's closest gay friends bitter about the way his family and the Redskins publicity office had handled news of the dying athlete's last days. In fact, among other business ventures, Jerry had owned and operated a gay bar in Austin, Texas, where for the first time in his life he had lived as an openly gay man. Had he crawled back into the closet as he lay dying, or was this the work of his family and closeted gays in the Redskins PR office? Nobody will ever know for sure, since the words in the interview were among Smith's last. But Smith's closest friends were saddened that the impression left by the article was that he had the courage to talk about AIDS but even on his deathbed still could not bring himself to talk about his homosexuality.

Kopay frantically tried to call Smith at the hospital, but by this time his family had closed ranks and were allowing no calls through. Kopay next called their old mutual friend, where Smith had been living, and the friend could only report the worst. "Believe me," he had said, "you wouldn't want to see him this way."

That night, Kopay sat down and wrote a long letter to Smith in which he told him how much he loved him, how everything he had managed to do was a direct result of his example and those long talks they used to have. Smith had often cited a little poem, "The Man in the Glass," as his code for living. In every one of the hundreds of speeches he gave as a celebrated athlete, Smith would always come back to the simple lines about being true to yourself, that no kind of success in life means anything if the man in the glass (mirror) is not your friend:

When you get what you want in your struggle for pelf [wealth]
And the world makes you king for a day,
Just go to the mirror and look at yourself
And see what the man has to say.
It isn't your father or mother or wife
Who judgment upon you must pass
The one whose verdict counts most in your life
Is the one staring back in the glass.
He's the one must satisfy beyond all the rest,
For he's with you right up to the end;
And you have passed your most difficult test
If the man in the glass is your friend.

The last ten years of his life, Smith had lived openly with a male lover. He had installed his mother, brother, and sister and their families in a compound of houses on the same property with his own house. Perhaps in this way Smith felt that he was being true to himself. But

An earlier shot of Smith, who struggled with his sexuality even after his playing days were over. Though he lived for a time as an openly gay man, the last articles that were written about him gave the impression that he was uncomfortable acknowledging his homosexuality in connection with his career and fame as an athlete.

during this time, including the two years he owned the gay bar in Austin, he stopped seeing all but one of his old football teammates.

Smith died within a few days after Kopay read the story in the newspaper. His funeral was as rigidly segregated as his life had been. Kopay felt compelled to get off work and fly to Washington for the service. Outside the church, he saw their old mutual gay friend across the way. The friend recognized Kopay, looked as if he had seen a ghost, and turned his back on him. (A year later, I was in the Redskins office doing research for an article about Jerry's life and death. There, in this friend's handwriting, were the plans worked out for the funeral. The former teammates who would serve as pallbearers were listed on the left—and off to the right beside a big question mark was the name "Kopay.")

Several of Smith's former teammates had been asked to serve as honorary pallbearers, but not Kopay. He sat off to himself at the back of the church as the teammates marched in and took their place in the front pews. He remembered the time when he had been one of them, marching in with Smith as a pallbearer at Coach Lombardi's funeral at St. Patrick's Cathedral in New York. Kopay looked at those around him and suddenly realized that, except for himself and the one older man Smith lived with, there was not a single gay person who had been part of Smith's life for the past ten years.

After the burial, there was an informal gathering of all the old teammates. It was obvious to Kopay that he would not be welcome, and he went off to spend time with some of his gay friends in Washington—just as Jerry Smith would have done.

In *The David Kopay Story,* Kopay had said he hoped that his example would create more space so that the next generation of homosexual athletes would not feel as entrapped by the stereotypes as he had been. He had every reason to believe when he wrote the book that he was only the first, that there would soon be any number of homosexual athletes unafraid to talk about their lives. But, surely in part because of the AIDS epidemic, that has not happened. Reporter Barry Meisel began his 1993 series on July 25 for the *New York Daily News:* "David Kopay is tired of being the poster boy for 'Gays in Sports.' Tired of peering into the same closet from which he emerged nearly 18 years ago and still seeing homosexual or bisexual athletes afraid or unwilling to go public."

The picture accompanying the *Daily News* story showed Kopay at work in the family store. He is older, wears glasses now, but still looks as fit as when he was a young athlete. More important, his face reflects a man at ease with himself. The man in the mirror is truly his friend now; he has a peace of mind that once seemed impossible in the days when he had been a bitterly confused young athlete.

Kopay's peace of mind was well earned; for some young athletes, similar feelings of confusion and isolation are much more destructive. For example, another young pro football player was so consumed by self-hatred and confusion that he came close to destroying himself in a suicidal accident. Ed Gallagher stood six feet six inches tall, weighed 275 pounds, was a champion weight lifter and football lineman in his hometown of Valhalla, New York. He went on to star for the University of Pittsburgh in the late 1970s and then went to training camp with the New York Giants. When he was cut after just two weeks, he went home to attempt to understand and unravel the hurt and confusion he felt about who he really was and who people thought he was. "I used to have a total fear of anyone suggesting I was gay back then," he told *Out* magazine in June 1994. "The word 'faggot' blasted in my head all the time. I didn't know how anything gay could mesh with my concept of what a jock was. If you were sensitive to helping little old ladies, you might get razzed about it. It was like sensitivity at all was anathema to being an athlete. It didn't mesh with the killer instinct you were supposed to have. And I certainly equated gay infatuations with sensitive nellie stuff."

Deep down, Gallagher knew he was homosexual, but he could not live with the idea of anybody knowing that. He was so consumed with guilt that he came away from every potential homosexual encounter feeling even worse about himself. Becoming more and more paranoid and suicidal, in 1985 he "fell" off the Kensico Dam in Valhalla, 12 days after having his first sexual experience with another man. As Barry

Meisel described it in the *New York Daily News,* "the fall fractured his neck and healed his soul."

Gallagher himself says, "When I came off the dam, I finally came to grips." He asked himself, "What the hell am I hiding anymore? I don't care." Though he will live the rest of his life in a wheelchair, unable to walk, "I was more emotionally paralyzed then, than I am physically paralyzed now," he says.

Gallagher now works as a volunteer counselor with a group called Alive to Thrive. He tries to work with younger people suffering from the same guilt and confusion he went through. He tells them that they are not alone and tries to save them from the same kind of "accident" that almost took his own life. Even so, he does not think that attitudes in big-time sports have greatly changed, and he does not believe that it would be any more possible for him to be out as a professional athlete in 1994 than it was in the late 1970s. "I don't think I could," he says. "It would have to be very clandestine."

Except for the backyard games of touch and flag, football is one sport that may never catch on in a big way with women. One likes to think that the liberated woman has better sense than to indulge in such a bruising activity—where serious injuries are a matter of course—and call it a game. From a purely practical standpoint, moreover, few women aspire to physiques of 200–300 pounds, which is almost a requisite for college and, in some places, even high school competition.

But in recent years millions of Americans, young and old, male and female, have taken up the older, more refined version of American football. This is a very recent phenomenon, but the "original" game of soccer has moved very quickly to a position of popularity with grammar school, high school, and college athletes—and it appears headed for increasing popularity in the years ahead. Soccer is a more graceful game than football, can be played by men and women alike, and relies not so much on bulk and brute force as on agility.

Although the few attempts to establish professional soccer leagues in the United States have been unsuccessful, around the world soccer is the most popular professional sport. Although there is only one professional player who is known to be openly gay, Justin Fashanu, who plays for a British team, the people involved in the sport do not seem to be as worried about their macho image as are American football coaches. In the United States, posters for the Rainbow League, the new soccer counterpart to Little League baseball, urge people of all sizes and all ages, "from three to ninety-three," to come out and have a good time playing or watching the game. Perhaps because it has been popularized in the U.S. by immigrant groups who have themselves felt the oppression of being minorities, the sport also appears to be more tolerant, more open to anybody who can and wants to play it—instead of requiring, as do baseball and football, for example, that one be of a certain physical size and strength in order to compete successfully. On a soccer field, particularly for younger players, little more is required than the ability to run and kick a ball, and the hulking giants who dominate football and basketball are easily outplayed by more agile, slimmer players, and even by sissies and girls.

4

The National Pastime

"The umpire is the loneliest man on the field," sportswriter P.C. Munson *has written. "At best, he is tolerated. More often he is ignored, and he becomes noticeable only as the object of fury and hatred for thousands of disappointed fans and a couple of dozen overheated ballplayers." As a closeted gay man, the loneliness of Dave Pallone, who umped in the National League for more than a decade, was even more acute.*

MORE THAN ONE OBSERVER of the American scene has said that if you would understand America, you must know baseball.

These were words for a slower, gentler time than now, however. Baseball is much too gentlemanly a sport to satisfy American audiences of today. The sport that once dominated the field as the American pastime is now often crowded out by faster-paced football and basketball, whose seasons get longer and longer, overlapping the spring and summer seasons once reserved for baseball alone.

Despite what the good folks in Cooperstown, New York, site of the Baseball Hall of Fame, have always said, there is some question as to whether Abner Doubleday (later an army general) invented the game of baseball there in 1839. Most historians agree that there were various forms of stickball in play throughout America long before this, one based on the English game of rounders, another called "one cat" or "two cat," and still another called "town ball" in Philadelphia and New York.

Whatever its precise origins, the game caught on fast once the diamond-shaped field came into use and rules were formulated at New York's Knickerbocker Club in 1845. There were baseball teams and games throughout the country a decade before the Civil War. The first amateur club was founded in New York in 1843, and the first professional club, the Cincinnati Red Stockings, was founded in 1868.

Baseball was, almost from the beginning, a professional sport, whereas football and basketball were closely identified with colleges. Though it's hard to imagine nowadays, there was a strong aversion among the sporting public to basketball and football when the players were being paid as opposed to being collegiate or amateur games that people played purely for the love of them. Many people felt strongly that introducing money into the equation would destroy the old "college spirit" of the games. It took decades for professional basketball and football to catch on and win the audiences they now enjoy.

But baseball was as American as the greenback dollar, and young boys throughout the land dreamed of making it to the major leagues and making some money in the process. In that sense, as in several others, the game partook of several aspects of the cherished American dream. Throughout its history, the game, on the professional level, has offered an opportunity for advancement and fame to the members of various immigrant and minority groups. The game requires no college education; nearly all of the players are hired straight out of high school, even today. And although it requires a high level of hand-eye coordination, baseball players need not be the outsize physical specimens who dominate basketball and football. More than the athletes in these other sports, baseball players seem more "normal" in a physical sense. For most Americans, the game, much more so than any other, is simply an indelible part of the culture.

If there is any minority whose history in the national pastime remains unwritten, it is gays. Simple statistical probability indicates that a significant percentage of the thousands of men who have played the game professionally over the years must have been gay, but if so, their identities have remained a secret. To this point, the names of just two individuals associated with the game on a professional level are known, and one of those was not a player but an umpire.

Whereas an NFL team plays just 16 games, at the rate of one a week, during the course of a regular season, a baseball team plays almost every day between April and October. Whereas a football game is played and then scrutinized afterward with an almost unbearable intensity, suggesting some of the seriousness of a military operation, a baseball game unfolds with much of the leisureliness of a sunny day, and the schedule progresses with the seemingly unhurried slowness of the sultry season in which it is set. No win or loss, no hit or error, no home run or strikeout, can be lingered on for too long, for there is another game tomorrow, and another the day after that. The progress of a player or a team is slow and cumulative. In football, a player who missed seven out of ten plays would be out of a job; in baseball, one who gets a hit three out of every ten times at bat will rank at the very top of his league, batting "three hundred" (that is, .300—and only an absurdly small number ever do that).

Perhaps because of the almost leisurely pace of the game, baseball fans and players are obsessed by statistics. Seemingly every move and gesture—even "errors"—are recorded, and the true fan can recite the most trivial statistics relating to the most marginal players and teams.

And so we come to one of those famous baseball trivia questions. Who was it who started the now-ubiquitous sporting custom of the "high five"? His name was Glenn Burke, and it happened on October 2, 1977, in a game between the Los Angeles Dodgers and the Houston Astros, the last game of the regular season in Dodger Stadium. Burke, a young outfielder with the Dodgers, was waiting in the "on-deck circle," the next in line to bat, when Dusty Baker hit his 30th home run of the season. This made the Dodgers the first team in major league history to have four batters hit 30 or more home runs in a season. As Baker came by him, instead of shaking his hand or patting him on the butt, Burke reached for the sky, holding up his hand for Baker to slap in a spontaneous gesture that came to be known as the

The burden of potential weighs heavily on many young athletes. For Glenn Burke, an extremely promising outfielder with the Los Angeles Dodgers in the late 1970s who was projected to be the next Willie Mays, it was an especially heavy load. A sense of self-confidence is absolutely critical to athletic success, and as a closeted gay man Burke always felt somewhat out of place with the Dodgers.

"high five" and is now standard reaction to an unusually good play in just about every sport.

In a recent interview, Burke laughed about his little contribution to the game's lore. "It's nice to leave your mark somewhere . . . besides the bedroom," he said.

That may sound like a peculiar allusion to one who does not know that Glenn Burke is, to this day, the only professional baseball player in the history of the game to be publicly identified as a homosexual, a designation that has far overshadowed his meager contributions as a player and his perhaps more significant gift to American popular culture. As he and countless others have learned, to be identified as a homosexual is to be known first and foremost by your sex life. You may be John Brown, who has climbed the highest mountain, hit the most home runs, or scored a winning touchdown, but once people know you are not heterosexual your achievements will be always prefaced with "John Brown, the homosexual. . . ."

Born and reared in Oakland, California, Burke was, like virtually all those who reach the major leagues, a teenage baseball superstar. By age 19 he was playing for a Los Angeles Dodgers farm team on the Triple-A level. (All 28 major league baseball teams maintain a network of minor league teams—often called farm teams—for the training and development of potential talent. These teams compete in leagues on several levels, from the so-called developmental or rookie leagues, which are for those who have never before played professionally on any level, on up the ladder from A to Double-A to Triple-A, which is the highest designation before the major leagues.) By age 23 he was a member of the Los Angeles Dodgers, whose coaches and scouts considered him one of the organization's most promising young players. "Frankly, we think he's going to be another Willie Mays," one of the team's coaches said of Burke, referring to the Hall of Fame outfielder for the New York and San Francisco Giants, who finished third on the all-time home run list and is generally considered one of the very greatest all-around players. Like Mays, Burke was considered to have "all the tools," in the parlance of baseball scouts. He was strong, fast, had the potential to hit for power and average, and was an exceptional fielder. Though not yet a regular member of the Dodgers' starting nine, Burke was an integral member of their pennant winning squad in 1977 as a late-inning defensive replacement and pinch runner.

Burke may have been an outstanding young man with a bright future in baseball, but he was also deeply troubled about his sexual identity. He had known for years that he was homosexual; he just did not know how to deal with it in public, particularly in the context of being a professional athlete. And so he behaved in a manner that must have seemed strange to his teammates, not to mention the coaches and owners. "I wasn't like the rest of them," he said in a 1993 interview. "I used to play ball and then go to my room and hide. The Dodgers wanted me to get married. Teams think if you don't have a wife and kids, if you're single, you're not stable enough and don't have enough responsibility."

In 1978, Al Campanis, vice president of the Dodgers, called Burke in for a talk. He said, "Everybody on the team is married but you, Glenn. When players get married on the Dodgers, we help them financially. We can help you go out and have a real nice honeymoon." Burke did not get married, and the next thing he knew he had been traded to the Oakland A's.

Only a year after he joined the team, halfway through the 1979 season, Burke was "released" (that is, fired), and he was out of baseball forever. He remains bitter about the way it happened. He is convinced the real reason was his homosexuality, although nobody ever told him this. "They never flat out told me why I was being released—and that's second class as far as I'm concerned. They certainly never said I couldn't play."

Whether that was the explanation for his brief career or not, Burke's career statistics—225 games played over parts of four seasons, with a .237 batting average and just 2 home runs and 38 runs batted in—indicate a player of exceedingly modest achievement. His greatest misfortune may have been the two teams—Los Angeles and Oakland—that he wound up playing for, not necessarily because of any organizational homophobia on their part, but because of the very high level of their on-field talent. It would have taken a newcomer far more talented even than the highly touted Burke to crack the starting lineup of the Los Angeles Dodgers of the late 1970s, a veteran squad that in Burke's years with the team twice won the National League pennant and was exceptionally well manned in the outfield, where two all-stars, Dusty Baker and Reggie Smith, played. (As a rule, young players generally, for obvious reasons, have a better chance of getting an opportunity to play and demonstrate their talent when they break in with a less successful team.) And although Oakland, which was firmly established in the American League basement when Burke arrived, would seem to have offered a better opportunity for him, the team was poised to climb back to the top of the standings, led by a trio of outstanding young outfielders—Rickey Henderson, Dale Murphy, and Tony Armas— who collectively were regarded as the league's best and left no room in the lineup for Burke.

Burke was still a very young man, just 26 years old, when he left baseball, with a whole lifetime and the possibility of another career still ahead of him. His immediate response to leaving baseball was relief, as if a great weight had been lifted from his shoulders. For years, as a ballplayer, he had felt that people were talking about him behind his back, saying, "There goes that faggot." Now he could visit the gay bars in San Francisco and Los Angeles and not worry about anybody seeing him. "I just started living my life, being me," he says. "I played softball, worked odds and ends. But I had no work experience. Every time I went for a job, it was, 'You don't have two years' experience.'"

To escape his loneliness, he had started taking drugs while he was still playing for the Dodgers. The drug habit escalated as Burke grew increasingly bitter about having been forced to leave the sport he loved. During one low time he was hit by a car; his leg was broken in four places and had to be reinforced with steel before he could walk again. In late 1993 he talked with Barry Meisel of the *New York Daily News* about trying to get off drugs. At that point, he was about as low as a man could go. He had no job, no car, no telephone, no address; sometimes, he said, he stayed with a stepsister back home in Oakland.

"I got cheated out of a career," Burke says. "That's what makes me angry. You know what? It drives me up the wall. Nobody really knows because I don't complain. But, yeah, it took a chunk out of my heart." Asked if he ever went out to the ballparks to watch the games now, Burke got all choked up and said no, he just was not able to do that.

He struggled to explain: "I have, I just have . . . I should be playing. I have some . . . some sentimental thing, I guess. It is tough."

As part of his struggle to regain control of his life, Burke began working with handicapped children in 1993. He knew what it was to be treated differently, to be a lonely outcast—and he had a lot of love

Umpire Dave Pallone, baserunner Vince Coleman, and shortstop Kurt Stillwell (from left) prepare for the pitch in the first inning of this August 1987 contest between the St. Louis Cardinals and the Cincinnati Reds. Even before allegations about his sexual conduct began to surface, Pallone had had a rough time as an umpire: He was ostracized by many of his colleagues because he had received his first job in the big leagues as a "scab" (a non-union replacement) during an umpires' strike in 1977.

to give. "It's amazing how much love kids need and how many of them don't get it," he says of the experience.

The baseball story of umpire Dave Pallone follows a similar line up to a point, but it has a happier ending because he did not resort to drugs and was able to talk back to his accusers and stand up for himself.

In pursuing a baseball career, Pallone was following not just his own dream but his emigrant father's as well. The elder Pallone, Carmine, was born in Pescara, Italy, and emigrated to Watertown, Massachusetts, with his own parents while he was still a young boy. He loved his new homeland and wanted to embrace everything American, especially baseball. The Pallones frequently went to see the Boston Braves play, and young Carmine became a passionate fan and a promising young player himself. By his late teens, he was such a good pitcher that the St. Louis Browns offered him a contract.

But this was during the height of the Great Depression, and the Pallones, like millions of other American families, were feeling tremendous economic pressure. Carmine Pallone's father said that there was no time to be wasted playing games. Instead, the boy went to work loading produce trucks for a dollar a day. The family's money problems endured, especially after Carmine had a wife and son of his own.

Dave Pallone remembers that his father was so determined to provide for his family that he would often put in a regular shift at a rubber-fabric factory and then work two other jobs after that and on weekends. Young Dave saw little of his father, but he never wanted for anything when it came to sports. He played basketball, football, and street hockey, but his great love was baseball, the same as his father's. There were rare but precious times when the father would take off from work and go with the boy to watch the Boston Red Sox play.

The father had an expensive baseball glove hidden high up in a bedroom closet. Dave knew it was there, but he knew better than to ask for it. In the meantime, he became such a passionate Red Sox fan that he would buy tickets for the games in Fenway Park two months in advance. He collected baseball cards and would fall asleep listening to the games on his transistor radio in bed. He would get so carried away that he would sometimes act out entire imaginary games in his backyard, playing all the different positions on the team himself, taking the parts of all his heroes. Once, he remembers, he even took the role of the umpire, called himself out, and then, after an argument ensued, threw himself out of the game.

Then the magic day came when his father brought down the sacred glove and passed it on to his son. He showed him how to take care of the glove and just how to hold it when he was playing. Dave was now more determined than ever to become a great baseball player, but at the time of his high school graduation, he was not good enough to play for a minor league team or to get a college scholarship.

He was floundering, trying to figure out what to do with the rest of his life, when he heard an announcer on the radio mention something about a training school for umpires. Being an umpire was as close as you could get to baseball without actually being a player. So Pallone set off for the school and passed through it with flying colors. He spent several hard years apprenticing as an umpire in the minor leagues and then, in 1977, received his first big break during a major league umpires' strike. Pallone and seven other minor league umpires were promoted to the big leagues.

To the union umpires he was a "scab," and he was never accepted by the older umpires, who would always resent him and his seven strikebreaking colleagues. But he had worked hard to realize his dream, and he could see his dream of officiating in a World Series on the horizon. One of Pallone's best-known calls involved a fracas with Cincinnati's Pete Rose, who before his banishment from the game recorded more base hits than any other player in history. There is a famous picture that shows the two men nose-to-nose yelling at each other just before Pallone threw Rose out of the game. Rose was suspended because of the incident—and Pallone had another powerful enemy determined to see him disgraced.

It was never anything but a rumor, but that was all that was needed. Pallone was supposed to have picked up another man in a bar in Cincinnati. He swears it never happened, but even if it had, he had not committed any crime, had not hurt anybody or shot anybody. Rumor or truth, it was enough for the commissioner's office to launch an investigation.

Pallone was beside himself with fear for his job. The commissioner's office was still reviewing the rumors from the Cincinnati incident when the killing blow came to Pallone's career. In 1988, when Pallone was 37, a story in the *New York Times* connected him to a sex scandal in Saratoga Springs, New York. The story was headlined, REPORT LINKS UMP PALLONE TO SEX SCANDAL. Several businessmen were accused of operating a "sex ring" with teenage boys in a private house in Saratoga Springs. Pallone says two of the men were friends of friends and that he had only visited the house in question twice, both times for a matter of minutes.

Like many people confused about or ashamed of their sexuality, Pallone, until a very late point in his life, had simply abstained from having sex with anybody. He had "fooled around" with other boys in high school, but thereafter had had no homosexual encounters until he was in his midtwenties. Meanwhile, he had made occasional attempts to have sex with women, but the two times he succeeded in "going all the way" only made him feel more confused about himself. When, however, at age 26, he met a young man on the beach in Puerto Rico and had sex with him, he knew that his homosexuality was for real, that this was who he was.

Still, Pallone kept to himself, avoiding bars or any place where he might be identified. For three years, he had a close relationship with a man named Scott. After Scott was killed in a car wreck, Pallone became so desperately lonely that he realized he would have to begin dealing with his homosexuality. He started going out to bars on rare occasions and planned to begin telling his colleagues and superiors in baseball about his homosexuality. The Cincinnati rumor and Saratoga Springs scandal brought a quick halt to his plans.

Pallone was brought before baseball commissioner A. Bartlett Giamatti, a former president of Yale University. Pallone thought he was going to get a fair hearing, but Giamatti told him he had only two options: resign or be fired. In a letter, Giamatti had accused him of "moral turpitude," a violation of his major league contract. Pallone says he always felt that Giamatti sympathized with his case but was forced into harsh action by others in the baseball hierarchy. After Giamatti's death, his wife told Pallone, "Dave, I just want you to know that Bart was very upset for months about your situation."

Major league baseball had called him out, but Pallone was not about to go slinking off, accepting his defeat in shame and guilt. He hired a team of lawyers, who successfully brought action against major league baseball. They proved that the rumors about the Cincinnati bar scene had never been substantiated. Also, the district attorney in Saratoga Springs had only mentioned that Pallone was involved. No charges against him were ever brought; and finally, in a tiny story nobody noticed, the DA announced that there was no evidence against Pallone.

Major league baseball finally agreed to settle the case with Pallone before it could be brought to trial. The terms of the settlement require that neither party ever publicly discuss it, but Pallone says it was more than he had asked for and enough for him to live very comfortably on for several years.

Meanwhile, Pallone (with the help of Alan Steinberg) had written a book, *Behind the Mask,* about his experiences. In the book he says, "It's time someone took the mask off baseball and shined the light on its real face. Baseball doesn't accept gays; and if what the game did to me is any measure of where it's headed, then it's going backward. I personally know of about a half-dozen gay major league baseball players—including some of the best-known and most accomplished players in the game—and the only problem they have is that they must lead double lives because baseball refuses to address the issue openly."

Because baseball, "hardball," was considered too dangerous for girls, we tend to think of it as the exclusive realm of boys and men. But this was not always so. There have always been a certain number of girls and women who wanted to get out there and play ball like the rest of the boys of summer. Once upon a time and not so very long ago, the girls and women had a league of their own—in fact, two leagues of their own. Lois Browne, a reporter in Toronto, Canada, heard about a reunion several years ago of the women baseball veterans and did a story about it for Canadian Television (CTV). She expanded the TV report into a fascinating book, *The Girls of Summer,* which was published in 1992 and inspired a Hollywood movie, *A League of Their Own,* starring Tom Hanks, Geena Davis, and Madonna.

The book focuses on the players in the All-American League, which lasted from 1943–54. The All-American League was the brainchild of

Tennis champion Billie Jean King throws the ceremonial first pitch in a 1976 Women's Professional Softball Association (WPSA) game. In addition to her achievements on the tennis court, King was a cofounder of the WPSA. Softball had long been regarded as an "acceptable," less strenuous and challenging substitute for baseball for women; by the 1950s, according to historian Lillian Faderman, softball leagues had become one of the few institutions available to young and working-class lesbians.

Philip K. Wrigley, who had inherited his daddy's chewing-gum business along with the Chicago Cubs baseball team. Wrigley, who had been phenomenally successful in business and with any number of little inventions, was frustrated by the unpredictable nature of the Cubs. Every three years, they would win the league pennant and then lose the World Series. He started the "girls" league as a wartime diversion while many of the best male players were in the military, but he seriously believed that the women players would one day rival their male counterparts in popularity.

From today's perspective, "girl" is hardly the word to describe a young woman able to compete seriously in a man's sport like baseball. But Lois Browne assures us that she reluctantly used that word because it was accurate for the times. The female players on Wrigley's teams were treated, as one recalls, "like chattel." They had male coaches and managers, and all decisions of any consequence were made by men. Although most were in their twenties, they were also chaperoned by older women.

The girls were paid only pennies compared to their male counterparts, and out of an enduring love of the game they put up with the absurd rules and regulations. Perhaps the most absurd was the requirement that they go through hours and hours of feminizing "charm schools"—this, mind you, after enduring full days of sweaty practice or actual games.

There had been some women baseball players and the rare all-female team as far back as the 1860s. With only a few serious exceptions, the female teams were regarded as comic relief from regular play, and the women who made the men's teams were extremely rare. A 17-year-old female pitcher made baseball history when she played with the Class A Chattanooga Lookouts in 1931. Her name was Jackie Mitchell, and she was brought in to pitch when the Lookouts played an exhibition game against the New York Yankees. It was a publicity stunt, for sure, but "the girl" did, in fact, strike out two of the most famous Yankees in history, Lou Gehrig and Babe Ruth. She also brought down the ire of the baseball commissioner, Judge Kenesaw Mountain Landis, who canceled her contract and opined that "life in baseball is too strenuous

Participants in San Francisco's Gay Softball League await the opening ceremonies that will signal the start of the 1993 season.

for women." In practice women were always barred from professional baseball, but that became an official rule in 1952.

In organizing his wartime women's league, said Philip Wrigley, "We will select the kind of players that people will want to see in action. Then we will groom them, to make sure they are acceptable. It won't be like the bad old days of peep shows and Bloomer Girls. . . . The League will be good for you and your community, good for the country, good for the war effort, good for you." The league's secretary added, "We do not want our uniforms to stress sex, but they should be feminine, with emphasis on the clean American sports girl."

The charm schools were conducted by none other than the cosmetics doyenne Madame Helena Rubinstein, who said the accent must remain on "neatness and feminine appeal. That is true of appearances on the playing field, on the street or in leisure moments." One of the best players, Lavonne "Pepper" Paire, says it was hard for a player to walk in high heels every evening when she had a charley horse from "busting our butts for ten hours on the field."

The feminine aspect was emphasized because the league was deathly afraid of any public suspicion that its players were lesbians—although nobody inside or outside of the league would ever have breathed that word in public in those days. According to Lois Browne, many of the best players were turned away because they looked too masculine; many others were sent home because of mere rumors of lesbian relationships or masculine behavior of any sort. It was an era when a woman could not be open about any kind of sexuality, and homosexuality was still the love that dared not speak its name. Engaging in homosexual acts was a serious crime throughout America.

Despite many precautions, Browne writes, some of the female baseball players were lesbians:

> The lesbian lifestyle (or, rather, its alleged outward signs) had long been a bugbear in ball-playing circles. When Connie Wisniewski began to pitch in Detroit in the early 1940s, she was told she would be kicked off the team if she chose to get a close-trimmed haircut. More than one All-American recruit who showed up at spring training with a boyish bob was handed her return ticket before she had even had the chance to warm up. Dottie Ferguson was warned by her chaperon against wearing girl's Oxford shoes because they were excessively masculine-looking. Pepper Paire endured "a lot of guff" in high school because she played ball. Her well-publicized success, and the publicity that surrounded her taking part in a tour to Mexico City, only made things worse. Even her teachers thought "it wasn't the thing for a young lady to do."

Browne mentions one coach who fired two women merely on rumors that they were lesbians, out of fear that they might "contaminate" the rest of the team. The men who ran the league "constantly protested too much, raising the spectre of same-sex preference even when it wasn't there. But homosexuality was as much a part of the 1940s as the 1990s. There were some lesbian players, and, chances are, chaperons. The fact of being lesbian was probably an added inducement to flee the stultifying atmosphere of their hometown and go on the ball-playing circuit."

A total of 550 women would play in the All-American League during its brief 11-year lifetime. If they did nothing else, they convinced their male detractors that women had the strength and skills to play the game almost as well as the men could. Dorothy Kamenshek, by all accounts the league's best all-around player, was given the highest accolade: a solid offer to play on a men's professional team.

Lois Browne includes a history of American softball in her book about women in baseball because that was where most of the players in the All-American League gained their experience. Softball, she explains, was invented on Thanksgiving Day, 1887, at Chicago's Farragut Boat Club. The outdoor baseball game had to be canceled due to rain, and George W. Hancock quickly thought of a game that could be played indoors. He fashioned a "soft ball" out of a rolled-up boxing glove and a bat from a broomstick.

The game caught on with the American public and was played by women from the very start. By the 1930s softball had clearly become the game most Americans participated in. According to a 1935 article in *Time,* more than two million people were then playing on 60,000 organized teams. One promoter in Chicago claimed that an all-female league of four teams had brought out 250,000 fans in one season.

Softball endures as the sport most Americans actually play. It is especially popular among gay men and lesbians and is one of the most spirited contests in the Gay Games. In Canada, the gay softball leagues are on a par with their straight counterparts. In her book *Odd Girls and Twilight Lovers,* Lillian Faderman writes that softball developed as a popular alternative to the sleazy gay bars that were for many years the only places where lesbians could find each other. "There were a few attempts by working-class and young lesbians in the 1950s and '60s to build institutions other than the gay bars. The most notable was the softball team. During those years many lesbians formed teams or made up the audiences for teams all over the country. Women's softball leagues usually had at least one or two teams that were all lesbian, and most of the other predominantly heterosexual teams had a fair sprinkling of lesbians. The games did succeed in providing legends and heroes for the lesbian subculture, as well as offering both participants and viewers some possibility for making lesbian contacts outside of the bars."

One young woman Faderman interviewed said, "Softball is the only consistent thing in this community. Political groups and social groups come and go, but softball will always be around."

Hundreds of gay and lesbian teams compete in various local leagues, in at least one national "world series," and in one of the most popular divisions of the Gay Games. In San Francisco, for many years the most talked-about game of the year was the annual police versus gay men's softball game. It had begun as a kind of grudge match when there were no openly gay members of the police force and when many gay people regarded the police as the enemy because of the many cases of entrapment and frequent raids on the gay bars. In recent years, when dozens of gays and lesbians who were also policemen or -women could have played on either team, the game has lost much of its tension.

5

Tennis

UNTIL IT REACHED AMERICAN shores, tennis was the "royal" game, played on "courts" in Europe. Nobody knows for sure what the word tennis itself means, but it was first used to describe a game with racket and ball in a poem written in 1400 in tribute to England's King Henry IV. In William Shakespeare's *Henry V*, the dauphin in France sends the king a present of tennis balls and Henry replies,

> When we have match'd our rackets to these balls,
> We will, in France, by God's grace, play a set
> Shall strike his father's crown into the hazard.
> Tell him he hath made a match with such a wrangler
> That all the courts of France will be disturb'd
> With chases.

France's famous Sun King, Louis XIV, who reigned from 1643 to 1715, was both a patron and player of tennis. The game was so closely identified with royalty

Bill Tilden raises the trophy signifying his triumph at the Men's National Championship tennis tournament at Forest Hills, New York, in 1929. It was the third time Tilden had won the championship.

and the nobility that it all but disappeared in France after the French Revolution (which had its beginnings, interestingly enough, in the so-called Tennis Court Oath—the demand for a constitution sworn by the members of the National Assembly on an indoor playing surface at the Palace of Versailles in 1789). Whereas at the start of the Revolution there were 250 courts in Paris alone, by 1879 there were just 6 in the entire country. The game remained popular among the upper classes in England, however, and was exported to the United States about 1874; by 1880 both the Boston and New York athletic clubs had built tennis courts as part of their facilities, and the first American national championships were conducted in 1881. By that time, the game was played mostly on outdoor courts made of grass. It was also one of the very few sports that women were allowed to compete in—so long as they were properly attired, of course. For many years, however, tennis remained a game of the upper classes, and it caught on only slowly with mainstream Americans. The 1911 *Encyclopaedia Britannica* noted that "the game is naturally played by comparatively few persons" in the United States.

In one of those bitter ironies of history, it would be a gay man who would take the "sissy" sport of tennis out of its precious upper-class setting and help to popularize it as an aggressive masculine sport. The man was Big Bill Tilden, who is considered by nearly all sports authorities as simply "the greatest tennis player of all time." Writing in *Sports Illustrated,* Frank Deford said Tilden "dominated tennis in his prime more than any man has ever dominated a sport." Likewise, it was a lesbian woman, Billie Jean King, who took the skirts off "ladies'" tennis and successfully fought to establish women's tennis on a par with male international competition.

William Tatem Tilden, Jr., was the most unlikely of sports heroes. Born to a wealthy Philadelphia family on February 10, 1893, he grew up in a mansion called Overleigh just two blocks from the exclusive Germantown Academy. He was tennis captain and class poet at Germantown, but even at this small private school he was far from the best player. At the University of Pennsylvania, he was ranked at the bottom of a not very good varsity tennis program.

Later, his school friends and family members would be amazed that this tall, thin, reclusive boy had ever made it as an athlete. After he dropped out of Penn one semester short of a degree, Tilden went home to his unmarried Aunt Betsy and Cousin Selena, the only family he had left after his mother died of a stroke, his father of kidney disease, and his brother from pneumonia—all within three years of each other while young Bill was still a teenager. He seemed to be making a career of staying alone in his room listening to opera records when Selena took him aside and told him he would end up just like her if he did not take control of his life, set some goals for himself, and get out of that old maids' home. Even after he became a successful tennis player,

Tilden instructs a group of aspiring young tennis players in some of the finer points of the game. Tilden came to prominence in the 1920s, a decade when the economic prosperity enjoyed by postwar America gave rise to a huge increase in the popularity of spectator sports. With Red Grange in football, Babe Ruth in baseball, and Jack Dempsey in boxing, Tilden came to personify the athletic achievements of the Jazz Age.

A champion falls: Tilden in a Los Angeles police station following his arrest in November 1946 for contributing to the delinquency of a minor.

Tilden would always say that his first love was music and the theater. He did, in fact, have a very brief career as an actor, and he would later write two novels, but these efforts would never compare in quality with his artistry on the tennis court.

Whether Cousin Selena's talk was the spur that kicked him out of the nest or not, it is a fact that within three years Tilden had moved up from being ranked as the 70th-best player in America to being the undisputed best tennis player in the world.

Unfortunately, the only biography of Tilden is written by Frank Deford, a senior editor at *Sports Illustrated*. The articles on Tilden by Deford that would eventually lead to the book reflect only one of the rare instances when *Sports Illustrated* has dealt with homosexuals in sports; the other notable time was when Dick Schaap wrote about the death of Tom Waddell, founder of the Gay Games. The magazine did not achieve its place as the premier sports publication in America by biting the hands that feed it. It is a magazine for fans, and it is written largely by reporters who are first and foremost fans themselves. They are not about to do anything that would demean the "heroic" (read heterosexual) traditions of sports. In the magazine's and Deford's view, Tilden's homosexuality was his "tragic flaw."

Deford was writing decades after Sigmund Freud's famous letter to an American mother declaring that while homosexuality was "assuredly no advantage," neither was it anything "to be ashamed of, no vice, no degradation, it cannot be classified an illness." By 1973 the American Psychiatric Association no longer listed homosexuality as an illness.

And yet Deford could write in the year 1976 that "Tilden's childhood reads like a textbook of circumstances liable to produce a homosexual male: the neglectful father who was devoted to another brother; the overprotective mother, warning her baby about the dirt and disease of sex." In the face of all kinds of scientific evidence to the contrary, Deford seized on now-discredited stereotypes about homosexuals and then strained to fit the facts of Tilden's life into the pattern. Deford frankly admitted to the *Advocate*'s interviewer, Randy Shilts, "I'm not putting myself up as an expert on homosexuality." He explained further that he had done little research on homosexuality because he had wanted to focus on Tilden's life.

But in telling us about Tilden's life, Deford perpetuates some of the worst myths about homosexuality. He writes that Tilden was homosexual because "he chose to be one, not because he had to." He quotes an infamous study that purportedly showed that 87 percent of all homosexuals were raised by overly possessive mothers and distant fathers.

Moreover, Deford makes the astonishing claim that Bill Tilden was the only great athlete known to have been homosexual. Even as he is writing about the daily terrors Tilden lived with, knowing about "the strange thing within him that society considered illegal and sinful," Deford apparently fails to understand why no other athletes—except for the two or three who had been arrested—were known to be homosexual.

In his first world title match at Wimbledon in 1920, Tilden lost the first set, 6–2, to the reigning champion, Gerald Patterson of Australia. But though Tilden had been dominated by Patterson in that first set, he nodded with confidence to an old friend in the stands as the players changed sides. And indeed, he soon took control of the court and won the next three sets. For the next six years, he lost no matches of any significance. Tilden's record includes three world titles at Wimbledon and seven U.S. championships. He also led U.S. teams to seven Davis Cup victories.

Tilden became an overnight celebrity, traveling like a prince in private railcars, staying in elegant suites at the most expensive hotels, visiting with presidents, cavorting with movie stars in Hollywood and real princes in Europe, celebrated along with football player Red Grange, baseball slugger Babe Ruth, and heavyweight champion Jack Dempsey as the greatest sporting heroes of America's rollicking Jazz Age. His entourage always included ball boys, with whom he spent much of his time. Deford would later propose a theory that Tilden was in search of the son he would never have and never had any erotic interest in the boys.

Tilden's arrogance had earned him a number of enemies in the tennis world. When word of his secret homosexual life began to spread, those enemies began a concerted effort to have him suspended from the American Lawn Tennis Association (ALTA). When Tilden was eventually suspended in 1928, the ALTA said it was because Tilden had taken money for writing a newspaper column about tennis and was therefore no longer an amateur. (Tennis at this point was still considered an amateur sport, played by gentlemen unsullied by competition for money.)

The tennis association's ruling caused an international incident because it came just before Tilden was to lead an American team in an effort to reclaim the Davis Cup, which the French had won in 1926. This had been billed as a historic rematch not just between the two national teams but between Tilden and his great rival, France's famed "Crocodile," René LaCoste (whose name endures as a result of the knit shirts still sold under his name with their famous emblem, not of a crocodile, but of a green alligator). In a rare moment of humility, Tilden had earlier said that the best he had ever played was in the match he lost in 1926 to LaCoste at the Germantown Cricket Club in Philadelphia.

Only after President Calvin Coolidge and the American ambassador to France intervened did the ALTA delay its suspension of Tilden so that he could face LaCoste in the spring of 1928 in a new stadium built to house this very match. Tilden was by this point in athletic old age at 36, and he was rated a two-to-one underdog for the match. But he was also fiercely determined. When LaCoste won the first set, 6–1, it looked like it was going to be an easy day for the Frenchman. But Tilden came back with LaCoste's own brand of vigorous all-out play and eventually triumphed in a grueling five-set match. Afterward, the defeated LaCoste, physically exhausted, told reporters, "Two years ago, I knew at last how to beat him. Now, on my own court, he beats me. I never knew how the ball would come off the racket, he concealed it so. I had to wait to see how much it was spinning, and sometimes it didn't spin at all. Is he not the greatest player of them all?"

In the worst days of the Great Depression, Tilden made huge sums of money as a professional tennis player. He may have been over-the-hill so far as the big championships were concerned, but people still turned out in numbers to see Big Bill play. Though still intensely closeted about his homosexuality, Tilden would on rare occasions (according to Deford) talk about it with friends, although this was more in the form of off-the-wall comments than any real heart-to-heart discussion. There was now no question that the ball boys were sleeping with him, and he would sometimes mention "cute" little things they had done in private.

When his cousin Selena took him to task for being so obvious, Tilden became furious and never spoke to her again. After relocating to Los Angeles in the early 1930s, Tilden moved among a wide circle of famous movie actors and actresses, his particular patrons being Joseph Cotten and Charlie Chaplin. He also "adopted" a family, a woman named Marrion Anderson and her son, Arthur. He would tell Marrion that Arthur was "the only real son I ever had" and would say to Arthur, "You and your mother are the only close family I ever had."

The Andersons were loyal to Tilden in his difficult later times when real family—if most of them had not been dead—might well have turned on him because of the public embarrassment he brought to the name. On the night of November 23, 1946, Tilden was arrested while driving his 1942 Packard Clipper in a very erratic manner down Sunset Boulevard. With him was a 14-year-old boy. Questioned by police, Tilden freely admitted to "indiscretions" with the boy on that night and the night before.

Tilden's lawyer tried to reason with him, but Big Bill's arrogance ruled. He refused to take the charges that were subsequently filed against him seriously and seemed confident he would never go to jail. But the judge was a hard-liner who had no sympathy for perverts or deviants, no matter how famous or successful. "Mr. Tilden," he asked, "have you ever given any thought, over the years that you have been engaged in athletics, to the harm that you could do if you were ever caught doing something like this?"

Billie Jean Moffitt displays her backhand form at Wimbledon in 1965. That same year she married Larry King and took his last name, by which she is still best known in the sports world.

Tilden replied, "Sir, I don't think I have thought of that because I have never been involved in anything of the kind."

The judge snapped back, "You mean you were never caught?"

Tilden answered calmly, "I mean I was not involved in it, sir."

Made furious by Tilden's denial, the judge sentenced him to a year at hard labor in the county jail. After that, he said, Tilden was not to be seen in the company of juveniles or he would be put back in jail. When Tilden's lawyer asked for a delay in execution of the sentence, the judge ordered it to begin immediately.

In fact, Tilden served his time (he was released for good behavior after seven and a half months) not at hard labor but as a storekeeper at Castaic Honor Farm just north of Los Angeles.

But when he got out, he found that most of his old friends no longer had time for him. Because of the sentence, he could not coach young people at tennis any more, which had been his only source of income once his playing days ended.

Down and out, he seemed as low as he could go when another blow struck. On January 28, 1949, Tilden and young Arthur Anderson were in his apartment alone—a clear violation of his probation—when police showed up with a warrant for his arrest on charges of having molested a young hitchhiker. The judge this time was more lenient; he ignored the more serious felony charges involving the hitchhiker, and on Tilden's 56th birthday sentenced him to another year at Castaic for violating his parole.

He was released early once more, on December 18, 1949, a matter of days before the Associated Press released a half-century poll on the greatest athletes of all time. Of all the athletes—Jack Dempsey in boxing, Babe Ruth in baseball, Jim Thorpe in football—Big Bill Tilden had been named number one in his sport by the widest margin.

His days of glory were gone, however, and all but a precious few of his old friends had turned away from him. His public image had always been that of a remarkably self-assured, if not downright arrogant, champion, but another side of his character was revealed by Sarah Palfrey Danzig, the two-time U.S. Open champion, who said, "Oh, God, you could see them snub him. He was so kind, so good. He deserved better from us all." One of his former protégés and closest friends said nobody rallied to his side, "myself included."

That was not exactly true; the Andersons were still there. And Gloria Butler, an old friend from Philadelphia, came out to help him find a place to live and resume his life; she even took an apartment in his building and stayed on for several months to help him through this harsh time. Though there were these few stalwarts who stood by him, Tilden's fame and the crowds and friends that went with it were all in the past. He died in his sleep on June 5, 1953, but not without hope. His bags were packed, and he had scraped together the money to go to the U.S. Professional Tennis Championship in Cleveland. He had decided, at 60 years of age, to go back and compete one more time. He was leaving for Cleveland the next day. A champion to the end, he surely died with dreams of hearing once more the roar of the crowd and standing one last time in the winner's circle.

Though there are still some major differences, by and large, women's tennis is now almost on a par with men's tennis in the world of sports. No other person has had as much to do with that development as Billie Jean King, a ferocious competitor on and off the courts.

She was born on November 22, 1943, the first child of Bill and Betty Moffitt, in Long Beach, California. As a girl, Billie Jean had considered her mother a very creative person, but it had been her father she had wanted to be like. He was a fireman in Long Beach, and from the time Billie Jean was a toddler he was her idol. He would slide down the fire pole with her in his arms. He carved her a bat, and—at least until brother Randy came along when she was five—Dad would spend hours hitting a ball and playing catch with young Billie Jean.

"I guess I was a tomboy in those years," Billie Jean wrote in her first autobiography, "although I wish there were a better word to describe little girls who happen to like sports." Her first love was football, but she also competed in softball, basketball, and track. She got her first taste of being a champion when she made "a shoestring catch of a looping line drive, then spun and threw to third base to double off a runner and save the game." Her teammates mobbed her as she came off the field, and she felt like the happiest little girl in the world.

Billie Jean Moffitt and Larry King at their 1965 wedding ceremony in Long Beach, California.

All this tomboy play was tolerated for a while, but then Billie Jean's mother finally put her foot down and said there would be no more football, no more playing games with the boys; it was "not ladylike." The "acceptable" sports for a young lady came down to golf, swimming, and tennis. Billie Jean thought golf was too slow, knew she would never be that good at swimming, and so chose tennis almost by default.

An old coach with the city recreation department took an interest in the 10-year-old when she showed up one day for tennis lessons. First lesson, he said, is "close the gate"—or you'll lose a basketful of balls.

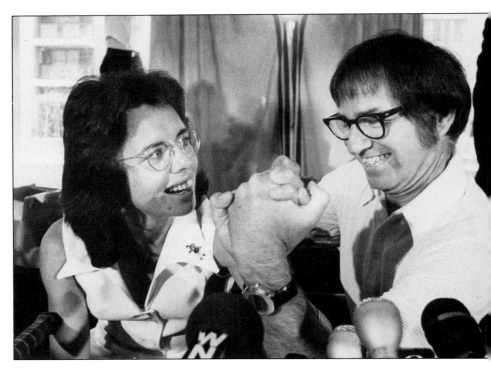

It is an indication of the relative lack of status of women's athletics in this country that for all her victories over numerous talented female opponents, King is perhaps best remembered for her 1973 victory over the aging Bobby Riggs (right, at a press conference prior to the match) in a match that was little more than a promotional gimmick. A former champion, Riggs by 1973 was a self-proclaimed tennis "hustler" who was long past his athletic prime.

He showed her the continental grip and taught her to drop the ball and then swing through it. She hit it the first time; from that point on, her life was enthusiastically focused on tennis. Her mother picked her up in the family car after that first lesson. "How was it?" she asked. "Great. Just great," her daughter answered. "I want to play tennis forever. I'm going to be the number one tennis player in the whole world."

"That's fine, dear," said her mother, continuing the drive home.

Though her parents, even her father, were not that big on sports, they were big on their two kids. They sacrificed so their daughter and son could have the sporting equipment they needed. They did without a new car and extra clothes. Her mother sold Avon products and Tupperware so that Billie Jean and Randy could keep up with their tennis and baseball.

Just nine months after that first lesson, Billie Jean entered her first competition, for the Southern California Juniors title. She lost that one, but that only made her all the more determined to win. The family pastor, a former Olympic pole-vault champion himself, asked her what she planned to do with her life and she answered, "I'm going to be the best tennis player in the world."

First she became the best junior women's player in Southern California, and then she began national competitions. By age 15 she was ranked number five in the country in her age group.

A moment in her early career left a scar, however, and King mentions it frequently. She had won her place as a junior champion in Southern California, but because she showed up wearing tennis shorts instead of the required skirt, she was prevented from appearing in that year's photograph of champions. That would rankle. She described the Southern California Tennis Association as a "regular male chauvinist den." She would write later that in 1970 the Los Angeles club offered women players "such a piddling share of the purse" that the women had to break away from the male-dominated associations and found one of their own. This was the birth of the highly successful Virginia Slims tour, and Billie Jean was instrumental in its creation. In the Women's Tennis Association that grew out of this breakaway organization, players are allowed to wear skirts if they want or plain shorts if they are more comfortable in them.

On September 17, 1965, Billie Jean married Larry King, a tall, handsome California blond whom she had met three years earlier at Los Angeles State College. He would go on to become her manager, and she gives him credit in her first autobiography for serving as a calming influence during her wildly successful climb to fame and fortune. He would be beside her in those peak moments of glory at Wimbledon; he would also be there during an all-time low point when a former lesbian lover sued Billie Jean for "palimony."

In her ensuing career as the world's best women's tennis player, Billie Jean would win 20 different singles and doubles titles at Wimbledon, a record still not bested even by the great Martina Navratilova. However, Billie Jean has said she is likely to be remembered in the record books not for her extraordinary performances in women's tennis, but for a circuslike match she played with Bobby Riggs, who had once been ranked the number-one male tennis player, although by the time of his match with King his star had long since faded. Though the match was essentially a gimmick—Riggs was more than two decades older than King and had been retired from the men's tour for many years—it was nonetheless billed as a "great battle of the sexes" and was staged before a boisterous crowd in the Houston Astrodome.

According to King, facing a man was difficult for her because of deep psychological reasons. The trouble, she says, was that "I was brought up a girl in a boy's world, and an awful lot of attitudes—prejudices—are locked within me." A similar set of fears and attitudes had undone her colleague and fellow champion, Margaret Court, whom Riggs had somehow managed to beat in a match several months earlier. King went into seclusion several days before her match in order "to help me get comfortable with the idea of beating a man."

When word got back to her that Riggs was playing at his best in practice sessions, King grew all the more nervous. She practiced her overhead return because she knew Riggs would be hitting lobs at her every chance he got. After days of hype, the two finally faced each other across the net. After the first set, they changed sides and she got a close look that showed her Riggs was just as nervous as she was. She realized he was vulnerable, too—and she went on to win easily the most sensational if not the most important victory of her career.

What many people remember about King's exposure as a closet lesbian was "the way she handled it"—that is, not very well.

She had met a woman named Marilyn Barnett, a hairdresser, at a Hollywood beauty shop. In the late 1970s, they became fast friends and eventually lovers. The relationship lasted for two years, and the two exchanged any number of letters during that time. They lived together as a couple in the Kings' Malibu beach house, which became Barnett's only home. Billie Jean was still married to Larry King, of course, and he stood by her when her former female lover started causing problems. The two women had grown apart, and Barnett had lived alone for several months in the Kings' beach house.

As the lovers' estrangement deepened, there were veiled threats at first from Barnett and then from her lawyers about going public with King's letters. Barnett's demands grew until she was finally asking for $125,000 cash and total possession of the Malibu beach house. Then she withdrew that demand and filed a so-called palimony suit (essentially a divorce action between unmarried long-term lovers), claiming that King had promised to take care of her for the rest of her life.

The judge agreed with the Kings and their lawyers that if Barnett's actions did not quite fit the legal definition of extortion, they came

A former hairdresser, Marilyn Barnett was King's friend, lover, and onetime manager. King admitted to having a sexual relationship with her, but she denied being a lesbian.

King in action at Wimbledon in 1975, the last year in which she competed individually in that prestigious tournament. Though King suffered economically as a result of disclosure of her lesbian affair, today she is remembered far more for her achievements on the tennis court than for her personal life.

awfully close to it, and the court ruled in King's favor. She may have won her case in a court of law, but in the court of public opinion she had lost a great deal of her reputation as a forthright and honest person. At a press conference King acknowledged that she had had the affair, but she insisted that she was not a lesbian and was devoted to her husband of many years. King said later that she thought she was "facing up to it"—treating the issue fairly and honestly—but to some it seemed more like she was trying to have it both ways: have a lesbian fling but still be thought of as straight, thereby trying to control the damage that could be done to her career and public image should she simply come out and admit that she was gay.

She wrote a second autobiography, which, oddly, she gave the same title as her first one, *Billie Jean,* almost as if she were filling in some spaces she had left blank in the first book. But even the second *Billie Jean,* written with Frank Deford, did not deal with her lesbianism except in an offhand discussion of labels and how destructive they are.

Before, King wrote in her second autobiography, she had felt that everybody respected her even though she was "a sweaty career woman." But after her lesbian affair became public knowledge, she admitted, there was a brief time when she was afraid to go out; she could feel people staring at her, judging her. Finally, she decided that the negative feelings were all coming from a very small number of people, "mostly that Moral Majority crowd that loves to quote Jesus . . . selectively. In my case, for example, I haven't heard any of them say, 'Judge not, lest ye be judged.'"

By her own estimate the news of her affair had cost her more than $1.5 million in contracts for endorsements, commercials, and lines of clothing using her name. She said that her husband lost an additional $400,000 in the businesses he was promoting because of the negative publicity.

In the second *Billie Jean,* King concluded a chapter by saying, "I must let my inner self be out front and free." But it is clear from the words she spoke in interviews following the palimony trial and the words she wrote in her autobiography—not to mention all the words that she could not bring herself to say—that she still had a long way to go toward that goal. She mentions with some bitterness in the book that a man who had had a similar fling with a woman would only find his career enhanced. True, but King was still not facing up to the fact that people now saw her as a lesbian, no matter how she saw—and described—

herself. She writes, "I have always disliked the labels that were arbitrarily placed on me, whether in feminist, heroic or less flattering terms." She failed to understand that a first step toward overcoming labels is to take them on and wear them and wear them out; to be able to say to people, "Oh yes, I'm a lesbian, but that's not all I am."

Though it is easy to criticize and condemn King's handling of her lesbian scandal, it is important to back off and consider her situation. Dealing with one's sexuality is difficult enough in private; to have to deal with it in public with little or no warning is an impossible situation that very few people could handle with grace. In fact, King's own experience justified her worst fears about the possible consequences of the matter. In addition to her own individual economic loss, Avon cosmetics threatened to withdraw its sponsorship of women's tennis altogether after the widespread publicity surrounding King's lesbian affair. In fairness to King, one should note that she never denied having the affair, and her own forthrightness on that score, as far as it went, most assuredly did help to create a climate of acceptance for the next generation of lesbian tennis players.

As King was putting her career back together, the brightest of all lesbian tennis stars was already rising out of Czechoslovakia and slowly but surely assuming dominance in women's tennis. Her name is Martina Navratilova, but her fame is so universal, she is that rare public figure who is known by one name alone: "Martina." She was born on October 18, 1956, in Prague, which was then the capital city of Czechoslovakia. Her mother and grandmother had both been local tennis champions. They were also members of a wealthy family that owned a grand estate that included apple orchards and several clay tennis courts. When the Communists seized power in Czechoslovakia in the late 1940s, Martina's family, like many other wealthy people, lost their property and were reduced to living in one tiny room of a house now inhabited by several families.

In a touching prologue to her superb autobiography—written with George Vecsey and published in 1985—Navratilova remembered her painful childhood in Czechoslovakia. "I was used to people mistaking me for a boy. I was the last girl in my class to get her period, and as for a figure, forget it. 'Scout,' an old lady once called me. 'Scout, could you help me across the street?' This time I saw myself in a full-length mirror and started crying. Big calves. Big ears. Big feet. 'I'm always going to look like a boy,' I cried."

Her father tried to reassure her: "'Don't worry,' he told me. 'You're a late bloomer. I can tell you're going to be pretty when you grow up.'"

This man whose name she bore and whom she called father was actually her stepfather. Her natural father had left her and her mother when she was three. Only later—during a dramatic confrontation with her parents in America—was Martina told that her biological father had killed himself.

But her stepfather took to her as if she were his own and instilled in her an early love for the sport of tennis. She writes that he "told me to play aggressively. Like a boy. I already did. Rush the net. Put it past them. Take a chance. Invent shots. He told me I would win Wimbledon some day. I believed that part."

Martina was 11 years old in the spring of 1968 when the people of Czechoslovakia began to rebel against the tyranny of the Soviet Union's overseers of their "puppet state." In January the hard-line Communist party leader was deposed, and Alexander Dubcek, a liberal reformer, was named to replace him. In February the Czech hockey team beat the Russians at the Winter Olympics, and even in the bitter cold, proud Czechoslovaks poured into the streets by the thousands to celebrate the 5–4 victory over their oppressors.

Fed up, in August the Soviet Union sent in 600,000 troops to subdue the Czechoslovak rebellion. In the aftermath, Navratilova wrote, she saw her country "lose its verve, lose its productivity, lose its soul. For someone with a skill, a career, an aspiration, there was only one thing to do: get out."

Clearly a promising young tennis star from an early age, Navratilova was allowed by the authorities to begin making trips outside Czechoslovakia at the age of 13, when she competed in a tournament in West Germany in 1969. Going anywhere outside Czechoslovakia was an adventure, but the place of her dreams had always been America, the land of freedom, sunshine, and all the money you needed to buy anything you wanted. Martina wanted it all, and she got her chance in 1973, when the Czech government agreed to let her play on the U.S. winter circuit.

As her plane left Prague that winter, the weather was bitterly cold, but it was sunny and warm as summertime when her plane touched down in Miami. Martina rushed out into the light of this dream come true. She was literally like a kid in a candy store, buying and eating so much in the fantastic fast-food and convenience stores that she gained 20 pounds in a matter of weeks. In 1975 she applied for and was granted political asylum in the United States, which meant that she could not return to her family in Czechoslovakia and which she hoped would lead to citizenship and permanent residence in the United States.

In her autobiography, Martina admits that she was woefully immature in her first years in America—and her tennis game showed it. However, with help from friends like the women's golf champion Sandra Haynie, she developed more poise on and off the court and learned the kind of self-control needed to win consistently. In 1978 she won her first Wimbledon championship, and the Women's Tennis Assocation ranked her as the number one women's player in the world, a position Chris Evert had held for the previous four years.

Martina was now a world champion tennis player, but there was still a part of her, in her own words, "that had never been touched before." Though she had had a few lesbian encounters, she thought nothing of them. "My self-image was that of an athlete, unconnected to the world of activism and meetings and writings and ideas."

She had read lesbian author Rita Mae Brown's *Rubyfruit Jungle* and liked it, but thought little more about it until she was invited to meet the author after a tournament in Virginia. Brown has described it as "the lunch that never ended." But Navratilova says that the two did not become romantically involved for almost another year. "There was something very direct, very aggressive, about her mind, something I had never encountered in a woman before," she wrote in her autobiography. "It was that seething, witty core that I was attracted to. She was the first person I ever met whom I could really talk to. Our

A young and exultant Martina Navratilova flashes a "v" for victory sign to the press in September 1975 after learning that she had been granted political asylum in the United States.

relationship wasn't all that physical to begin with, but I was attracted to her emotionally and especially intellectually."

When Navratilova's parents came to visit, her father suspected that Martina and Rita Mae were more than just friends, and fierce shouting matches ensued. In the heat of one of these arguments with her parents, her mother told her about her father's suicide and said, "You're just like him." Her parents had come to America with the idea of staying, but after the arguments over Martina's lesbianism, they became determined to go home to Czechoslovakia. Through it all, Martina was understanding and forgiving of their intolerance. With the money she gave them, they were able to build a grand hilltop house on a small estate. They took the money, but they have never accepted their daughter's sexual identity.

Meanwhile, Navratilova had paid $500,000 for a home of her (and Rita Mae's) own—a beautiful old antebellum house with a nine-acre estate in Charlottesville, Virginia. She may have been stimulated by the intellectual life with Brown, but Navratilova was also increasingly concerned about her physical training and her increasingly inconsistent tennis game. After a match in Florida, she had met a professional women's basketball player named Nancy Lieberman, who seemed the answer to all her needs of the moment. Lieberman was a blunt-spoken person who promised to whip Navratilova back into shape with a rigorous daily workout regimen. In short order she moved into Lieberman's townhouse in Dallas, but not without a farewell fight with Brown that remains legendary among gays and lesbians.

Apparently it is not true that Brown stood firing a pistol at her as Navratilova sped off in one of their Cadillacs, but the scene contained

Eleven years after being granted asylum in the United States, the results of Navratilova's commitment to a rigorous physical conditioning regimen are evident as she lunges during the Virginia Slims championship in New York City in November 1986.

just about everything but a loaded gun. Navratilova describes it as "one of the nastiest, most physical arguments I ever hope to be in."

In 1981, with the public disclosure of Billie Jean King's lesbian affair, Navratilova grew terrified that her own lesbianism would become public knowledge. She still did not have U.S. citizenship, and she lived in constant fear that she would be sent back to Czechoslovakia and never get out again. Her lawyers advised her to apply for citizenship in California, where the examiners might be more tolerant if the question of her sexuality should come up.

To qualify for citizenship, she had to write a sentence in English and name the first president and the current chief executive. She answered in the negative to oral questions about drugs and a criminal record. "There was also something very quick about my sexuality, and I just gulped and said I was bisexual, and she never even glanced up from the form she was reading, just went on to the next thing." The examination was held in May; in July her lawyer called to say she was now a U.S. citizen. "I was so thrilled because now I could finally unpack my emotional luggage and really feel at home."

Not long after she obtained her citizenship, Navratilova got a call from a reporter for the *New York Daily News*. Several months earlier, she had talked with him about her relationship with Brown and her fears about what publicity about her private life might do to her career. The reporter told her he could no longer hold off publishing the interview. By that time, there had already been so much speculation and gossip that it was hardly news that Navratilova was a lesbian. Still, it was a historic moment in the history of gays and lesbians because Navratilova, as the result of the conditioning regimen with Lieberman in Dallas, was about to begin the period of her most dominant tennis. For many years to come she would be the only openly gay athlete in a major sport competing in the United States, as well as arguably the greatest champion in the history of her sport. By the time of her retirement in late 1994, Navratilova had won more major singles titles than any female player in history.

Navratilova acknowledges that being open about her lesbianism has cost her a great deal of money from endorsements, but many of the sponsors that she already had did not drop her over this news. And even without big-time commercial endorsements, she has earned more than $15 million in regular tournament purses.

After her autobiography was published in 1985, Navratilova seemed to think that there was no reason why she should ever have to talk about her private life ever again. She left Lieberman and Dallas for the comparative peace and quiet of Aspen, Colorado, where she lived with her new spouse, Judy Nelson. As one reporter observed, if she had not actually gone back into the closet, she had moved "into a very private bedroom with all the windows carefully curtained."

But in the early 1990s, the venomous antihomosexual crusade in her adopted state forced Navratilova to choose between her desire for privacy and the obvious fact that she could be a powerful force if she stood up for gay and lesbian rights in the face of this campaign. In 1992 voters in Colorado passed Amendment 2, which allowed discrimination against homosexuals. The legislation inspired a nationwide boycott of the state by many individuals, and it made an active and potent political force out of Navratilova, an athlete who never before thought much about politics. She spoke out against the antihomosexual forces in Colorado, and she has addressed dozens of rallies since then. She was the most-quoted speaker at the massive Gay and Lesbian March on Washington in 1993, and she was the chief spokeswoman, the real-life poster girl, for the 1994 Gay Games in New York, though a previous engagement at Wimbledon kept her from attending the games themselves. At 38, when most athletes have already retired with their trophies, she was still a contender—in tennis and now in her private life as well.

The crowning moment in Navratilova's career, on and off the court, came at an elaborate gay and lesbian tribute to her at Madison Square Garden in New York City on July 28, 1993. With Navratilova as the main attraction, this single event raised more than $250,000 for the Gay Games. And there stood Billie Jean King beside her throughout the evening. One can only speculate on the private anguish that King had endured to reach the point where she could take such a public stand. "As a friend," said King, who is 13 years older than Navratilova,

Judy Nelson (in stetson) congratulates Navratilova after her win in the quarterfinals at Wimbledon in 1988. A Texas housewife and mother of two sons, Nelson fell in love with Navratilova in 1984. That year, the two were "married" in a Methodist church in Brisbane, Australia. Their relationship ended in 1991, and Nelson subsequently became involved with another one of Navratilova's former lovers, Rita Mae Brown.

"Martina has helped me understand my own sexuality. I've had many struggles with it over the years. One thing I love about Martina is that she demands acceptance on equal terms for all of us. Not tolerance, but acceptance. Because she is comfortable in her own skin, she helps all of us be more comfortable in ours."

When it finally came Navratilova's turn to speak that night, she said, "When I get all these accolades for being true to myself, I say 'Who else would I be?' I can't be Chris Evert."

6

The Olympics

*Come, stranger, try thy skill in sports, if haply thou art
practiced in any; and thou art like to have knowledge
of games, for there is no greater glory for a man while yet
he lives than that which he achieves by hand and foot.*

—Laodamas of Phraecia to Odysseus

*But even if one should win a victory by swiftness of foot, or
in the pentathlon . . . or in wrestling, or in painful boxing,
or in the dread struggle which men call the pancratium, and
should win a conspicuous seat of honor at athletic contests,
and should receive his food at public expense, and a gift
which would be a treasure to him; yes, even if he won a
victory with racehorses . . . though he should gain all this,
he would not be as worthy as I. For wisdom is better than
the strength of men and horses . . . and it is not right to
honor strength above excellent wisdom.*

—Xenophanes of Colophon

*An ancient sculpture of
a discus thrower from the
original Olympic games.
In ancient Greek society,
homosexuality was not
viewed as being incompat-
ible with masculinity, and
sexual relations between
males were not regarded
as abnormal.*

HOMOSEXUALITY WAS VERY MUCH a part of life in
ancient Greece because it was then, is now, and always
has been a part of nature. John Boswell and other

classical historians have pointed out that the Greeks did not merely tolerate same-sex lover-warriors, they made heroes of many of them.

In an article in the May 10, 1993, issue of the *New Republic,* Boswell wrote that the idea for democracy in ancient Athens is believed to have begun with male lovers named Harmodius and Aristogiton. From that point on, homosexual love was identified with personal freedom and democracy: the two men had waged an early battle for human rights against the tyrant who had tried to come between them. Boswell quotes Plato's reflections on this: "Our own tyrants learned this lesson through bitter experience, when the love between Aristogiton and Harmodius grew so strong that it shattered their power. Wherever, therefore, it has been established that it is shameful to be involved in sexual relationships with men, this is due to evil on the part of the rulers, and to cowardice on the part of the government." Indeed, one of the most famous and most feared of the Greek fighting forces was the Sacred Band of Thebes, composed of 300 men, 150 pairs of male lovers.

The famous athletic games conducted by the ancient Greeks on the plains at Olympia are generally dated from 776 B.C. to A.D. 393. This was the time of the Olympiad, four-year periods coinciding with the games. However, the games are believed to have started even earlier than this. If one cannot fix a definite date for the Olympic Games' beginning, historians do know the specific date of their ending—A.D. 393, when the Roman emperor Theodosius the Great, a Christian, prohibited the games scheduled for 394 and ordered all of the "pagan" buildings at Olympia destroyed. Determined to make his own sect of Christianity the world's only religion, Theodosius suppressed not only those who worshiped the ancient gods, but those whose brand of Christianity did not agree with his own.

The Olympic Games remained dead for 1,500 years. Some attempts were made in England to revive them in the early 1800s, but it was largely through the work of a Frenchman, Baron Pierre de Coubertin, that a successful attempt was made to revive the games as a form of international competition. The first games in the modern cycle were staged in the restored stadium at Athens in 1896; they have been held every four years since, although they were suspended during

World War I and World War II. The modern Winter Olympics started in 1924.

Like the original games, the modern Olympics hold an almost sacred place in the sporting world. Not merely to be the best in one's league or state or even country but to be honored as the best in all the world in your chosen sport is the young athlete's highest, most improbable dream.

In the nearly 100 years since the modern games began in 1896, there have doubtless been many hundreds, maybe thousands, of participating athletes who happened to be homosexual. Until the last decade, any competitor who had become known as homosexual, privately or publicly, would have been sent home. As elsewhere in sports, rigid homophobia still prevails in the Olympics. However, in recent years several Olympic athletes have come out of the shadows and talked about their homosexuality, the most prominent being the American athletes Bruce Hayes, a swimmer; Tom Waddell, a decathlete; and Greg Louganis, a diver, who officially came out during the opening ceremonies of Gay Games IV. Their examples will surely lead to greater space in the athletic world for others to be open about their homosexuality.

Hayes remembers watching the Olympics on television as a boy of nine. "I thought, 'Wow, if only I could do that.'" He set himself a grueling six-hour-a-day schedule and by age 10 was already a national champion. After attracting national attention as a swimmer for the Highland Park High School in Dallas, he was awarded a swimming scholarship to the University of California at Los Angeles (UCLA).

Hayes set his sights on the Olympics and began the rigorous daily training that would be required for several years, embarking on a one-dimensional life that absorbed all his youthful energies. Only later would he be able to look back and wonder if maybe he was not trying to compensate for his homosexuality through athletics, proving to himself and the world that he was a real man. He dated women a few times, but his few sexual experiences with them were not at all satisfying to him. Unable to respond the way that he felt he should to women, he kept thinking that maybe he was asexual.

Widely regarded as the "best ever" in his event, diver Greg Louganis won gold medals in the 1976, 1984, and 1988 Olympic Games. Louganis came out publicly at the Opening Ceremonies of Gay Games IV in New York City in 1994, but he does not believe that homophobia in bigtime sports has greatly diminished. "While I haven't competed since 1988," he told a reporter from Out *magazine in June 1994, "from what I hear it's not much better today than it was years ago, and it was no picnic then."*

"I was so focused," he says, "my head was in the water." During the time he was in training for the Olympics, he had no sexual experiences with men. "I was in denial. If you would have asked me, I would have said, 'No.'"

At the Pan American Games in 1983, Hayes dominated the 200- and 400-meter events, beating the American champion Rowdy Gates in the process. This accomplishment earned him a place on the cover of *Swimming World* magazine. The accompanying story quoted a coach saying Hayes "is going to let somebody go by him over his dead body." He had remarkable strength and seemed to do best as an underdog, coming from behind in the last 50 meters.

At the 1984 Olympics the anchor position was the key to winning the 800-meter freestyle relay, but nobody on the American team wanted to be the last man in the race; that was left to Hayes. That meant a fierce race to the finish against West Germany's powerful Michael Gross, known as "The Albatross" because of his long arms. Hayes recalls, "Even the other three guys were like, 'Omigod, I don't want to anchor.'"

The race was close the whole way, but as Hayes and Gross headed for the finish, it looked like a photo finish. Just before the wall, Hayes gave an extra kick and surged slightly ahead, giving the Americans an upset win by a mere .04 seconds. The crowd in the swimming stadium went wild, and Hayes came home an all-American hero. He and the other three members of the relay team were featured on the cover of *Vanity Fair* magazine.

Having achieved his goal as a swimmer, Hayes now decided that he had had enough of the one-dimensional life. He left UCLA and international swimming competition and completed his undergraduate work at Northwestern University in Chicago, where he earned a B.A. in journalism.

Once he had left behind the intense existence of the Olympic competitor, Hayes felt free to explore his true sexual feelings. "As soon as the Olympics were over," he says, "all that started coming to the surface. We're talking a matter of days." He began going to bars, making new friends, and enjoying the sexual life he had long denied himself.

He had a difficult time explaining himself to his parents for a while, but they listened and learned and, after a brief break, ultimately resumed their relationship with the young athlete who had made them so proud.

Hayes's first choice for a career had been journalism, but when it came time, he decided he just was not aggressive enough to be a reporter. Instead, he joined one of New York's most prestigious public relations firms. He also joined Team New York Aquatics, the gay swimming team. That move, he says, "really helped me integrate the two sides of my life, the gay side and the swimming side."

Hayes had come out to his parents and a few friends, but it was not until he entered Gay Games III in 1990 in Vancouver, Canada, that he began speaking out publicly about being homosexual. Needless to say, he was extremely successful at the Gay Games, winning seven gold medals.

Competing as an openly gay man was "a hundred percent better" than his previous athletic life, Hayes said. Before, he had lived in constant fear that he would be ostracized by his teammates if his secret became known. "I was just very frightened," he remembered. But the Gay Games, he says, "was in many ways the most satisfying and most gratifying experience in my athletic career." He has become one of the most active spokesmen for the Gay Games. "Hopefully," he said, "we'll shatter some of those stereotypes that gay people aren't athletes, because we are."

Surely the most extraordinary figure in gay athletic history is Tom Waddell. He had that rare mix of physical charisma, strength and kindness, wisdom and compassion, that touched other people's lives and changed them forever. *Los Angeles Times* reporter Robert Scheer described him as "a tall, muscular Greek-god type." The *Advocate*'s Ron Bluestein recalled seeing him in 1976 and thinking, "Tom Waddell was the most beautiful bloom of a man I had ever seen, period."

Most fascinating of all was the response of Dick Schaap, one of the deans of sports journalism in America as a newspaper reporter and columnist, author of numerous sports books, and television journalist. Schaap first met Waddell when he was assigned to do a story on him for ABC Television's "20/20" program. By the time, months later, that

Waddell died from AIDS, the two men had become close friends, as Schaap reported in a touching article for *Sports Illustrated*. "I knew him for only seven months, but he may have been the most impressive human being I ever met," he wrote. "Certainly he was the most impressive athlete. He combined strength and sensitivity, intelligence and courage, compassion and competitiveness, in dazzling doses. He contradicted all the stereotypes of both the athlete and the homosexual."

Waddell was born Tom Flubacher in 1937, the child of a poor working-class German Catholic family in Paterson, New Jersey. His father drove a bus, his mother ran a delicatessen. They separated when Tom was a teenager, and he eventually moved in with another couple in the neighborhood, Gene and Hazel Waddell, who loved and nurtured him as both son and protégé. When they legally adopted the Flubacher boy when he was 21, he took their surname.

Gene Waddell had at one time been a member of a tumbling act that made front-page news by doing a dangerous balancing act on top of the Empire State Building. After that act dissolved, Gene met and married Hazel, and the two played the vaudeville circuit as an acrobatic act. He coached young Tom in gymnastics; she taught him dancing.

Tom first dreamed of becoming a dancer, and as a teenager he studied ballet for a brief time in New York. But after another male dancer propositioned him, he fled the dance scene and dedicated his life to sports. He set a high school record in the high jump, and his overall abilities earned him a scholarship to Springfield College in Massachusetts.

Springfield was a "phys. ed." college, and Waddell aspired to becoming a track coach until a tragic accident in the gym changed the whole course of his life. He and his roommate, Don Marshman, were known as the Gold Dust Twins because they were such superb athletes and cocaptains of a gymnastics team that won nearly every meet in New England. Marshman was a premed student who had talked often with Waddell about his hopes of becoming a doctor, of serving mankind, but his dreams were cut short one day when the two were working out in the gym. Marshman was practicing giant swings on the high rings when he lost his grip and plunged headfirst to the floor. Waddell rushed to his friend's side. Blood trickled from Marshman's ear as Waddell held him in his arms. A last look of terror crossed Marshman's eyes, and then he was dead.

Waddell was so devastated by the loss that he determined to adopt his friend's cause and become a doctor himself. Meanwhile, he continued to excel in college athletics. He made the All-East team in football, but his real talent lay in track and field. At one track meet, against Amherst, Waddell alone scored more points than the entire Amherst team.

Waddell had known from a very early age that he was homosexual, but he said that somehow he was never plagued by the self-hatred common to so many other homosexuals. "I liked who I was. I liked what I felt. I didn't want any of that to change. But I didn't want to be this bizarre social and physical outcast. I wanted to be liked. I wanted to have lots of friends, and I realized the way I was going to do that was . . . through an athletic capacity, that came easily to me."

There were a few brief homosexual encounters during his college years, but Waddell had no real love relationship with another man until the summer after college, when he was working at a children's camp in the Berkshires. There, he met and fell in love with Friedrich Engels "Enge" Menaker, who operated a nearby camp for adults.

On its face, it was a highly improbable match. Tom was only 21, and more involved in sports than politics, where, if anything, he considered himself an Eisenhower Republican. Enge, on the other hand, was 63 years old and a devout socialist. He ran "The Farm" as a haven for intellectuals. He was a liberal of the old school, and he shared his love of opera, art, and literature with his new young love. The one issue Menaker was less than liberal on was homosexuality. A product of his times, when being openly gay was the equivalent of committing professional and personal suicide, he believed that no one who publicly revealed his homosexuality could be held in high regard by others.

Waddell would later tell the *Advocate* that he had wanted to come out when he first fell in love in 1960. "There were so many things about this person that I loved and admired. I was so happy, I wanted to come out. The man I fell in love with was 63 and of course, his whole gestalt about homosexuality was molded by having been born in 1895." Menaker told him, "You must never, ever tell anybody that you're homosexual. It'll ruin your career." Menaker had internalized societal attitudes that portrayed homosexuality as "anathema to clean living, something to be ashamed of. He really bought the prevalent attitude."

Swimmer Bruce Hayes receives a teammates's congratulations after winning the gold medal in the 1983 Pan-American Games in Caracas, Venezuela. For Hayes, none of his many accomplishments in athletics have been as satisfying as his participation in the Gay Games.

Waddell never did. "On a personal level, I've always wanted to come out because I hated living a lie. I felt it was damaging me in some very basic ways to live that lie, to have to deny in subtle ways that I was a homosexual. 'When are you getting married?' 'Well, I haven't met the right person yet' instead of saying, 'I don't intend to get married because I can't marry another man.' I hated being closeted. I didn't want to be. I felt this was a restriction on my freedom and I would not be liberated until I could not think of being perverse." After that summer in the Berkshires, Waddell would go on to other lovers in other places, but his love for Menaker endured, despite their differing attitudes on homosexuality, and the two remained close friends until the older man's death in 1990.

Like Bruce Hayes, Waddell maintained a dream of representing the United States at the Olympics. In college, he had placed 10th in national standings for the decathlon, a series of 10 difficult track-and-field competitions, conducted over 48 hours, that many regard as the ultimate athletic challenge. The highest laurels at the ancient and the modern Olympics have traditionally been reserved for the athlete who finishes first in this event. Waddell worked hard at improving at it, but when he tried out for the three-man U.S. Olympic decathlon team in 1960, he still finished 6th.

Waddell then focused his energies on medical school. He earned an M.D. in 1965, served an internship, and then, with the United States committing an increasing number of troops to the war in Vietnam, had to face the draft. Denied status as a conscientious objector because of his atheism, Waddell was drafted into the army in 1966. He was stationed at Walter Reed Hospital in Washington as part of an international medical program. There he was also able to resume training for the decathlon, and he became, at 30, the "old man" on the U.S. decathlon team at the 1968 Olympics in Mexico City.

As being in the Olympics was something he had wanted to do for his entire life, Waddell said, "I just put the sexual part of me on the shelf while I was doing it." Others on the Olympic team "were all heroes to me. I just had to keep pinching myself. Is this real? I can't believe this is really happening to me. It was ecstasy."

As he marched into the stadium in Mexico City with the U.S. team, Waddell felt like the happiest man alive. "I felt like a rock and roll star. I'm strumming away on my guitar and everyone's going crazy for me." Waddell was actively involved with the black American athletes who intended to use the Olympic Games as a forum to make a public statement in support of "black power." He met with them "in solidarity" behind the scenes, helped draft statements, and agreed with them that whoever won anything would give the black power salute as "The Star-Spangled Banner" was played. This earned him the enduring ire of the ultraconservative U.S. Olympic Comittee (USOC). Waddell, of course, was still in the army and was actually threatened with a court-martial by the USOC's Don F. Miller. (Meanwhile, black sprinters Tommie Smith and John Carlos, who won the gold and silver medals, respectively, in the 100-meter dash, were stripped of their medals and sent home by the USOC for having bowed their heads and given a clenched-fist black power salute during the playing of the national anthem after the medals were awarded.)

There was no active or overt homosexual activity that he knew about among the Olympic athletes, Waddell said later. "There's very little homosexuality in sports in terms of orgasm," he explained later. "But there's a lot of game-playing. There's a lot of hugs and ass-slapping—but it's all done in a very masculine context. It's like when they say, 'Hey, you caught a nice pass,' and then follow it up with a slap on the ass. O.K. That's very masculine, but why did they pick the ass to slap him on?"

Waddell believed that many athletes were driven into athletics not in spite of their homosexuality but because of it. "Many athletes use sports as a smokescreen. They're doing things that will make them the most masculine—the big jock."

Waddell came in sixth in the decathlon competition at the 1968 Olympics; the winner was another American, Bill Toomey, who would later travel with Waddell on track-and-field exhibition tours in Africa and South America. In the world of American sports, Toomey was the champion of all champions, the ultimate athlete, the complete macho man. And yet Toomey was in awe of his older colleague's uncommon

Tom Waddell puts the shot at the 1968 decathlon national championship in Santa Barbara, California. As a decathlete, Waddell had to excel in 10 separate track-and-field events.

energy and his humanity. "Many days, after I was long gone and tired, Tom would go to a local hospital and work all night on patients with tropical diseases."

After the army, Waddell held a number of medical positions that gave him a chance to travel around the world. He served as a medic on a research ship, then worked for two years in Saudi Arabia as an adviser to the royal family and as the architect of that country's national sports program. He continued training for the decathlon and even set a new record for 34-year-olds in 1972. The next year his competitive sporting career came to an abrupt end when he twisted his leg while pole-vaulting and severely damaged his kneecap.

Waddell may have been out of the running so far as the Olympics was concerned, but he was still an athlete at heart. Moreover, he was becoming more and more active in the gay community, increasingly concerned about making a lasting contribution. In 1976 he and his lover, Charles Deaton, were the first homosexuals ever featured in *People* magazine's "Couples" section.

In the end, he would contribute one of the most popular and enduring events in international gay life. In doing so he would combine the best of two of his worlds, of being an athlete and being homosexual. He would plan and organize a Gay Olympics, a quadrennial festival for gay athletes. There was already a Senior Olympics and a Special Olympics and any number of other Olympics, but the sporting officials on the U.S. Olympic Committee went berserk at the idea of a Gay Olympics; their chief spokesman was Don F. Miller, who had once tried to "arrest" Tom Waddell at the 1968 Olympics. The fight over the name proved long and expensive, but the Olympic Committee finally (with the blessing of the U.S. Supreme Court) succeeded in blocking Waddell's use of the word "Olympics."

Undeterred, Waddell proceeded with his plans for the Gay Games. Beginning with just a few hundred athletes at first, the event would grow into a major international sporting convention. What Waddell would discover was that there was an unbelievable number of gay athletes out there who had chosen a different alternative to mainstream straight sports, and they were all just waiting for a chance—not so much to compete and win, but just a chance to play, like all the heterosexual athletes had long been able to do. In coming together for their own games, gays and lesbians would create an international festival far more successful than any of them could ever have imagined—and, in doing so, they would also succeed in restoring some of the more wholesome aspects of sports that had been lost in the cutthroat world of professional athletics.

7

Gay Alternatives

IN A "SPORTS SPECIAL" issue of the *Advocate* in 1984, editor Robert McQueen recalled a painful story from his childhood that reflected the experience of nearly every gay man and plenty of lesbian women in America.

As a tiny, slightly rotund six-year-old, McQueen stood among other boys waiting to see who would be chosen for the Little League baseball team. Suddenly, McQueen heard the captain's voice above the din of the playground. He was looking at McQueen and shouting so everybody could hear: "We don't want a fairy on our team."

McQueen hardly knew what the word "fairy" meant, but the boy knew from the way the captain said it that it was bad, really bad. He sat stunned with mortification, desperation, and terror for a few seconds. Sweat broke out on his forehead, his eyes started burning with tears. Then, McQueen remembered,

Gay hoopsters pursue a rebound at Gay Games III in Vancouver, British Columbia, in 1990.

By the 1990s, gay and lesbian athletes in the United States had devised their own counterparts to virtually every straight sporting institution. Here, two members of the New York Knights, a gay wrestling team, grapple during a training session at the Gay and Lesbian Cultural Center in New York City.

"'Run,' said my six-year-old brain to my stubby, somewhat awkward six-year-old legs. 'Run before they see you cry.' And run I did, never to return willfully or comfortably to the little league macho world of boys' sports where 'fairies' were not welcome."

Another gay man's Little League memories were also recorded in that issue of the *Advocate*. He was forced to play by his father, and he has bitter memories of never fitting in. "They always stuck me in the outfield and I always sat down and picked at the flowers. I couldn't relate to the competitiveness and macho mentality. I just didn't feel like I belonged."

But the happy ending to this man's story does not lie in a contemplative life away from the playing fields. At age 33, he had been able to go back to sports and found—much to his amazement—that without the societally imposed stress of his earlier experiences, he loves it. "If somebody had told me when I was first coming out that I would become a jock, I'd have told them they were nuts. When I decided to join the gay softball team, it was as if I'd resolved to break the final taboo in my life. I was afraid I would be laughed off the field. Instead, I met a terrific group of people who were totally supportive and eager to help me improve." In addition to the softball team, he was also a member of a gay volleyball team and a gay running club, and he worked out in a predominantly gay gym.

McQueen remembers growing up and learning about the world of "fairies." He says,

> I did my best to fit into their world. I learned about opera and interior decorating, high fashion and show biz, all the things gay men were supposed to be interested in. "Camping" in this community was not a rugged weekend in the mountains, and "athletic" referred to how you performed in bed. Still, I cycled, skied, swam, hiked and took gymnastics classes, but almost always alone. It just never occurred to me that my gay friends might want to go along.
>
> Then I witnessed something I never thought I would see. A gay softball team was pitted against the San Francisco police all-stars in a now traditional game complete with cheerleaders and noisy spectators, most of whom were gay. What's more, the event was covered in the daily papers and the proceeds went to a recognized charity. This time, however, I didn't have to run from the field. I was with people who understood—my own people.

The new popularity of sports among gays coincides with the growing gay political awareness and the growing sense of gay pride in recent years; it also coincides with the international AIDS epidemic, which, in America, has had its most devastating effects among homosexuals. Beginning with safe-sex campaigns, gay leaders, especially physicians, have gone on to emphasize the importance of good health in general in the gay community. This has led to an increasing awareness of physical fitness, not just for the good looks that go with a good body, but for the health benefits that accrue to the physically fit individual as well.

Just as other minorities throughout history have formed their own organizations and institutions, gay athletes have found each other and organized leagues of their own when they were turned away from—or were made to feel unwelcome on—the more traditional heterosexual teams. This was the subject of a paper presented in April 1989 to the American Alliance for Health, Physical Education, Recreation and Dance by Brenda G. Pitts, a sports administration professor at the University of Louisville. The paper was entitled "Leagues of Their Own: Organized Responses to Sport Homophobia." In her study, Pitts examined 132 gay sports organizations throughout the country. In every case, she found the primary reason for creating the leagues was escape from the antihomosexual attitudes in the nongay leagues.

The gay softball and volleyball leagues were so successful and so fiercely competitive on a national scale that they found themselves having to deal with problems similar to those the larger society has faced in its treatment of homosexuals.

Originally, the National Gay Softball Association had tried to set a 20 percent "quota" on the number of straight players allowed on a gay team. The Community Softball League in San Francisco was especially proud of its mixed teams, and Mayor George Moscone had issued a proclamation in honor of their efforts. Moscone claimed that "in San Francisco, there's more understanding between straights and gays and all ethnic groups, because they play together. Sports are the best way—there's a great deal of togetherness." But in 1978 San Francisco found itself disqualified from the Gay Softball World Series for having too many heterosexuals on its teams. Mark Brown, commissioner of the Community Softball League, said, "They cry for human rights, but how are they going to get them if they don't let straight people know them?" Eventually, gays would organize yet another league of their own in San Francisco, outside the jurisdiction of the National Gay Softball Association, and the National Gay Softball Association would stop the quota system in favor of an outright ban on straights in gay softball.

At the 13th annual Gay Softball World Series in Atlanta in August of 1989, there was yet another heterosexual scandal in gay softball, as the sport was once again "tainted" by straight players trying to invade the gay locker rooms. At first, there was only gossip. An official of the North American Gay Amateur Athletic Alliance (NAGAAA) assured reporters, "We feel fairly confident that there are no nongay players. The Gay Softball World Series is a place to showcase gay ability. If people went back to their own cities after the series and said, 'San Francisco won the gay world series, but it was a straight guy who hit the winning home run' . . . that is not what we are trying to accomplish."

The city of Los Angeles features a gay hockey league. In March 1993, several members followed the action on the ice as their teammates took on a rival squad composed of members of the Los Angeles Police Department.

But that is precisely what happened that year in Atlanta. The host city's own Bulldog Lushpuppies lost to New York's Break Falcons, 17–1. But the losers protested because the New York team had a nongay player. The NAGAAA commissioners ruled in Atlanta's favor, and New York forfeited the game. One commissioner explained that the suspect player "was married with two kids and when we asked if he was gay—out of the closet—he could not say yes. Some people think this is a tournament to bring people out of the closet, but that is not true. This is a homosexual tournament."

Meanwhile, the New York coach vowed to challenge the ban on nongay players. "If five NAGAAA officials can determine whether a player is gay or straight, then I'd like to see the test. It's decided solely on the whim of the protest committee."

Only in the team sports, where the teams often are sponsored by bars or other businesses and compete nationally, have issues like these become a problem in the world of gay athletics. Having felt the effects of discrimination themselves, most gay and lesbian athletes are careful, when forming their own groups, not to discriminate against anybody.

The president of the largest gay sports group, the International Gay Bowling Organization, says, "I'm not aware that any of our member leagues discriminate. We've had people chairing national committees who were not gay." The Arcadia Bodybuilding Society, which hosts the National Gay and Lesbian Bodybuilding Championships, is open to everybody with no restrictions regarding age, race, sexual orientation, or anything else.

Surely the most unexpected and most successful of the gay alternatives to straight sporting events is the most macho of all American activities of any sort, the rodeo. The first gay rodeo was staged in Reno, Nevada, in 1975. From fairly small beginnings, the International Gay Rodeo Association has now expanded to include rodeos in six different cities every year. The 1993 schedule took the show to the East Coast for its first rodeo in the nation's capital, Washington, D.C.

Greg Olson grew up in a rodeo family in Phoenix, Arizona. "My whole family was involved in rodeos when I was growing up. But I stayed home and looked after the animals. It seemed like my brothers were gone every weekend at some rodeo, but it really didn't interest me. It seemed too redneck." Being gay, he felt he would never fit into the redneck rodeo scene.

Then he heard about the Arizona Gay Rodeo. "It was kinda a lark. A friend needed somebody to compete with him in one of the camp events—the wild drag race. After that, I wanted to get involved. It musta been in my blood." Olson became a frequent competitor on the gay rodeo circuit and became one of its stars in bull and bareback bronco riding, winning All-Around Champion Cowboy three years running.

In addition to regular rodeo events such as bull riding, bronco busting, calf roping, and barrel racing, the gay rodeo offers opportunity for a whole new cast of cowhands with its wild drag races, steer decorating, and goat dressing events. One of the champion barrel racers, Joyce Myers, says, "I've competed in both gay and straight events, and this is just as tough. This is no different." (Unlike the straight rodeos, all of the gay events are open to women.) Olson disagrees somewhat with Myers, holding that the rougher events are not on a level with the regular rodeos, but that is not the point. "I'd say the gay rodeos are on a competitive level with high school rodeos," he says, "but the atmosphere is entirely different. I really feel out of place at straight rodeos. Here it's great. We're gay and together, and nothing else matters."

Many of the gay groups have shunned not only straight teams and participants but the whole idea of what "sports" means to most heterosexuals. The Houston Outdoors Group has 250 members who regularly engage in hiking and camping trips designed to provide an alternative to the gay and lesbian bar scene. The Lavender Winds Kite Club in Vancouver meets for kite flying once a month. In New York the Sundance Outdoor Adventure Society organizes hot-air ballooning events. In Toronto more than 600 Canadians belong to Out and Out, a parachuting group. In Boston gay and lesbian bicyclers have organized the Out Riders club, whose motto is "out of the bars and onto the roads." Unusual Attitudes is a Southern California group of 150 gay and lesbian pilots. There are gay and lesbian scuba-diving clubs throughout the country, from San Diego's Finny Dippers to the Village Dive Club in New York to the Sea Snakes in San Francisco. Lori Cruz, a diving instructor from Santa Cruz, California, says, "It's truly a buddy activity. The macho male image of diving has been replaced with a new 'Let's go and explore' sensibility."

Bob Underwood of the Tarheel Outdoor Sports Fellowship in North Carolina sings the praises of canoeing in a swamp with a group of gay men: "Sometimes we're in groves overhung with Spanish moss, poling through cola-dark water or canoeing through thick mats of duckweed, and we hit a stump underneath the water, or a beaver dam. Or there'll be snakes as big as my arm all over the place. It gives you a real jolt. If you're adventurous and with other people who like to challenge themselves, there's a whole lot of mutual bonding that goes on. It's the way to go for gay people who have not felt welcome in team sports."

The most well-known gay sporting alternative by far is the Gay Games. Tom Waddell's plan for a gay Olympics caused a good many people, gay and straight, to look askance when they first heard about it. To some, it sounded a lot like little kids playing dress-up in clothes that did not fit. Some felt embarrassed at what sounded like a pathetic attempt by gays and lesbians to imitate the real games. The underlying assumption seemed to be, "If you won't invite us to your party, then we'll just have a party of our own." But to many, the idea of a gay Olympics just did not sound right, for it could never measure up to the original. Or so it seemed.

Mariah Burton Nelson was just one among 1,300 athletes from around the world who marched into Kezar Stadium in San Francisco for the first Gay Games in 1982. She had been a star basketball player in college and had been a member of two pro teams; she had known athletic success in the "real" world. Nelson has written about what she felt that morning:

> I felt a little silly at first, and waved to the hordes of people in the stands sheepishly. But the roar of their approval enveloped me and their clapping and cheering overwhelmed me; for the first time in my life, I was cheered not for swimming fast or putting a ball through a hoop but for being both athletic and honest. . . . What made the experience euphoric was the sense of freedom. In high school, college, and professional athletic contests I'd participated in, the fear of being thought gay had restricted even sponta-

This pool hall in Brooklyn, New York, attracts a large lesbian clientele for its popular "ladies' night" features.

neous expressions of emotion; at the Gay Games, in contrast, women gave each other loving unhurried hugs after triumph or disappointment or simply out of affection. Men held hands. The lack of homophobia was like a welcome blast of fresh air—or like nitrous oxide, making everyone giddily happy. It was a taste of what could be; a gathering at which everyone, regardless of skill, could pursue excellence, where competitors could encourage each other, and where athletes could be caring and demonstrative without hesitation.

The idea for an international gay Olympics sprang naturally from the wide-ranging experiences of Dr. Tom Waddell. Olympic athlete, physician, humanitarian, Waddell felt a personal responsibility to contribute to the world around him and, along with that, an obligation as a member of the gay minority for his people to make a larger contribution to the rest of the world.

"If we're going to be an exemplary community," he said, "if we're going to teach the society at large, we need to confront issues of racism, ageism and sexism that still plague us. The primary purpose of sport should be self-fulfillment, but athletics can also be a powerful medium for social change."

Waddell had an enormous credibility factor to overcome in getting support for the games; he got little support from inside the gay community and almost none from outside. "People looked up and said, 'Gay Olympic Games. Well, uh, what does that mean? High-heel races?' We had to get across the idea that this is a very serious event. And it was very slow to sink in."

The first time Waddell tried to solicit funds, he was bitterly disappointed by the response. The mailing had cost more than $5,000, but only $1,200 came back. Then word started to spread, and Waddell's spirits were lifted, especially by the responses he received from gay athletes in foreign countries. More than 19 foreign countries would eventually be represented in the games.

Not one to give in to adversity, Waddell persevered, and the games proceeded as scheduled. The opening day was August 28, 1982. The acting mayor of San Francisco, City Supervisor Doris Ward, defied the Olympic Committee's ban and declared it "Gay Olympics Day" in the

city. Ward said, "Throughout history, people have been afraid to acknowledge gay participation in sports. You can shout it now—the athletes are here."

The 1,300 athletes were led into the stadium by two former members of U.S. Olympic teams, carrying a torch that had been carried across the country from the site of the Stonewall Riot in New York City in 1969, which is generally regarded as the beginning of the

Soccer, the world's most popular sport, is also a favorite at the Gay Games. At Gay Games IV in New York City in 1994, athletes competed in 31 different events.

modern gay rights movement in the United States. The torchbearers were George Frenn, a member of the 1972 U.S. track team, and Susan McGrievy, who was on the 1956 U.S. swimming team.

The opening ceremonies included a rousing set by Tina Turner and a moving anthem written for the games and sung by Meg Christian. A cultural festival of art exhibits and other events was staged to coincide with the games. At the closing ceremonies, a chorus of

700 members of West Coast gay and lesbian singing groups would raise their voices in a new "Song of Victory" and "Torches in the Wind."

Writers Rita Mae Brown and Armistead Maupin were masters of ceremony for the games. Brown had some harsh words for the closeted professional athletes who make millions of dollars "lying about being gay." And she had high praise for those who had come to participate in Gay Games I. "You have your integrity and honor," she told them, "and you carry ours as well. When we look at you, we see the best that we can be."

One of the proudest winners in the swimming competition for people aged 36 to 45 was San Francisco deputy sheriff Douglas MacDonald. He won firsts in the 50- and 100-yard backstroke, the same events he had won the previous month at the International Police Olympics in Austin, Texas. (The U.S. Olympic Committee did not object to the use of the Olympic name by the police.)

What everybody would remember most was the spirit of the games. A typical scene took place in the wrestling preliminaries. The two male wrestlers fought long and hard. Their bodies soaked with sweat, they were nearly drained of energy when one of them finally pinned the other's shoulders to the mat. The loser lay back and breathed a deep sigh of resignation. The winner leaned over and kissed him.

"The events were competitive and at the same time supportive, exhilarating, loving and caring," said one of the participants. Richard Boner, who won six individual and team gold medals plus a silver medal for diving, said, "The last place competitor gets the most applause because he or she had the guts to do it."

The first Gay Games broke even financially, but just barely. Though the games had been successful from many different perspectives, the biggest crowd, at the closing ceremony, had been only 10,000, a number that constituted only a small percentage of the available seats in huge Kezar Stadium. Waddell could only think of all those empty seats as he and others began planning for Gay Games II. He said they needed to "refine" the program a bit there in San Francisco before farming it out to other cities.

America's most popular participant sport, softball, is also represented at the Gay Games. Here, a player from New Zealand swings for the fences at Gay Games III.

More than twice the number of gay and lesbian athletes responded to the call for Gay Games II, leaving Waddell ecstatic. After the long and bitter struggle over the word "Olympics," he now said that he agreed that the word would have been inappropriate for the Gay Games: "Let's look at the Olympics. The Olympics are racist, the Olympics are exclusive, they're nationalistic, they pit one group of people against another, and only for the very best athletes. That doesn't describe our

Games." In "our Games," he continued, "winning's not important, doing your best is important."

Waddell served as president of the San Francisco Arts and Athletic Association, which sponsored the games, but the overall planning and organization was done by Shawn Kelly, executive director for Gay Games II. It was Kelly who approved the slogan, In August, 1986, Something Wonderful Will Happen . . . For the Second Time. The second games were especially notable for the high level of participation of women, both in the executive offices where the planning and

More than any other individual, the Gay Games are the legacy of Dr. Tom Waddell, seen here at Gay Games II holding his daughter, Jessica.

organization was done and in the athletic competition itself. In the weight-lifting events at the second games, for example, the women contestants outnumbered the men three to one.

San Francisco's mayor, Diane Feinstein, addressed the opening ceremonies of Gay Games II: "One of the things that has been a privilege for me to see in San Francisco is the spirit and the talent that rests within the gay community, both men and women. Special spirit, special talent, a coming together in times of trial. And that spirit must continue."

Once again, author Rita Mae Brown was master of ceremonies and she, too, spoke of continuing the spirit of the games. "So these Gay Games are not just a celebration of skill, they're a celebration of the best in us. It's a celebration of courage because all the athletes, whether straight or gay, had to overcome a certain amount of prejudice. They had to brave public opinion to come here. If *they* can do it, *we* can do it.

"I applaud each of you for being here. I know you have had an individual journey that's all your own, and it was often painful. But you're here, we're all together, we're one family and we're all we've got. So I say, 'Come on, we're all in the same boat, let's pick up an oar and row.'"

With twice as many athletes competing and the crowds at all events much larger than at the first games, the ailing Tom Waddell could look out with pride on all that he had created.

He attended the second Gay Games with what he described as his own greatest achievement in hand, a beautiful four-year-old daughter named Jessica whom he had fathered with a lesbian athlete named Sara Lewinstein. Although one could not tell it by looking at him, he was dying of AIDS, having been diagnosed just four weeks before the game with Pneumocystis carinii pneumonia, tragic news that many in the audience were aware of as they watched him accepting a plaque declaring him "Papa Games" at the closing ceremonies.

The angry words of author Armistead Maupin, who once again spoke, touched the heart of everyone who had ever known Tom Waddell or stood by helplessly watching a friend or lover die of AIDS:

"When we speak of gay pride, our pride is not really in being gay, but in telling the truth about it—telling it loudly and telling it often, because so many have lied about it for so long. These lies have fostered an ignorance so enormous that preachers and presidents have stood idly by and clucked their tongues while thousands of good men were dying. I would like to tell you that the death of these people has meant something. I would like to believe that their bravery has made us braver people, has opened our hearts and taught us to value truth."

But, Maupin continued, there were still antihomosexual homosexuals whose "self-loathing translates into misery and misunderstanding for honest lesbians and gay men everywhere." The operative word was "gay," not "Olympics," Maupin concluded. "The operative word is honesty, not athleticism. A gold medal here doesn't mean a goddamn thing if you have to keep it out of sight when you get home."

Within a matter of months, Papa Games Waddell would himself be another number among the growing death statistics for AIDS. Dick Schaap wrote that Waddell faced death as he had faced life. In his last days, he busied himself seeing that his finances were in order for his daughter, Jessica, and that all his work at the Gay Games was taken care of. And then, on July 11, 1987, he calmly crossed his hands in his lap and said what he must have known would be his last words, "Well, this should be interesting." "Tom Waddell was quite a man," Dick Schaap wrote in *Sports Illustrated*.

His spirit lives on through what most people saw as an absurd, impossible dream when he first started talking about it in 1980. Waddell had been such a powerful, relentless force behind the games that some wondered how they would be able to continue after his death. Some made dire predictions that without Waddell the games themselves would soon die.

But the spirit was too strong for that; too many thousands of lives had been touched by Waddell and the first two games. An enormous Canadian maple-leaf flag was raised at the closing of Gay Games II because Vancouver had been chosen as the next site of the games. The Metropolitan Vancouver Athletics and Arts Association hired Shawn P.

The placards waved by these participants in Gay Games III indicate the breadth of the event's appeal. Forty countries, from six continents, were represented at Gay Games IV.

Gay athletes rehearse their roles in the opening ceremonies of Gay Games IV, the most successful of these quadrennial events to date.

Kelly to be the consulting executive director and to continue what he and Waddell had started in San Francisco.

In Vancouver the number of participants and viewers of the Gay Games once again doubled. More than 7,000 athletes competed, 700 in soccer alone; and more than 20,000 fans watched the opening and closing ceremonies. Perhaps more important to the future of the games, the city of Vancouver estimated that the games and the accompanying arts festival had pumped more than $30 million into the city's businesses.

In fact, three years later then-mayor of New York City David Dinkins would estimate that more than $100 million would be spent by spectators and participants in Gay Games IV in New York in 1994. The New York games coincided with a massive gay demonstration in honor of the 25th anniversary of the Stonewall Riot, when gays in Greenwich Village had fought back against policemen conducting what they no doubt regarded as just another routine raid on a gay bar. The Gay Games were just one part of a yearlong celebration of gay pride in New York called the Unity '94 celebrations.

When one looks back to that first fund-raising attempt in 1982 by Tom Waddell, it is clear that the Gay Games have come a very long way in a very short amount of time. At just one of hundreds of fund-raisers for Gay Games IV—a tribute to tennis star Martina Navratilova at Madison Square Garden—more than $250,000 was raised. What would have seemed even more incredible to Waddell and others involved in gay sports just 10 years earlier was the backing given by several corporate sponsors for the 1994 games. Though that sponsorship is still far short of the money spent on mainstream sporting events such as the Super Bowl, it is a whole lot more than nothing, which is all that gay groups had ever received before. "The Gay Games are without question the most inclusive event in the world, boasting five times the number of athletes who participated in the '92 Winter Olympics," David Dinkins said in welcoming the selection of his city as the site for the games.

What is clearly a new day in the history of gay people will perhaps also mark a new beginning for sports. Having seen what sports has done to homosexuals over the years, it might now finally be possible to see what homosexuals can do for sports.

◨ *Further Reading* ◨

Brown, Rita Mae. *Sudden Death*. New York: Bantam, 1983.

Browne, Lois. *Girls of Summer*. New York: HarperCollins, 1992.

Faderman, Lillian. *Odd Girls and Twilight Lovers*. New York: Columbia University Press, 1991.

King, Billie Jean, with Kim Chapin. *Billie Jean*. New York: Harper & Row, 1974.

King, Billie Jean, with Frank Deford. *Billie Jean*. New York: Viking, 1982.

Kopay, David, and Perry Deane Young. *The David Kopay Story: An Extraordinary Revelation*. New York: Arbor House, 1977.

Lefcourt, Peter. *The Dreyfus Affair*. New York: Random House, 1992.

Marble, Alice, with Dale Leatherman. *Courting Danger*. New York: St. Martin's Press, 1991.

Michener, James A. *Sports in America*. New York: Random House, 1976.

Navratilova, Martina, with George Vecsey. *Martina*. New York: Knopf, 1985.

Nelson, Mariah Burton. *Are We Winning Yet?* New York: Random House, 1991.

Pallone, Dave, with Alan Steinberg. *Behind the Mask*. New York: Viking, 1990.

Sabo, Donald F., and Ross Runfola. *Jock: Sports and Male Identity*. Englewood Cliffs, NJ: Spectrum, 1980.

Warren, Patricia Nell. *The Front Runner*. New York: Plume, 1974.

❖ *Index* ❖

Advocate, 19, 85, 112, 114, 121
AIDS, 53, 54, 56, 113, 123, 135
All-American League, 77, 78
Arcadia Bodybuilding Society, 126
Are We Winning Yet? How Women Are Changing Sports and Sports Are Changing Women (Nelson), 28

Barnett, Marilyn, 94–95
Baseball, 61–78
    homosexuals and, 61, 66, 76–77
    women and, 73–78
Basketball, 27, 34–38, 59, 62
    homosexuals and, 13, 34–37
Behind the Mask (Pallone and Steinberg), 73
Billie Jean (King and Deford), 97
Boner, Richard, 132
Brown, Rita Mae, 100–102, 103, 132, 135
Browne, Lois, 73, 74, 75, 77, 78
Buck, Tina, 25, 26, 27
Burke, Glenn, 63–70

Christian, Meg, 131
Community Softball League, 124
Conradt, Jody, 37

David Kopay Story: An Extraordinary Self-Revelation, The (Kopay and Young), 47, 52, 56

Deford, Frank, 82, 84, 85, 87

Faderman, Lillian, 78
Fashanu, Justin, 58
Ferguson, Dottie, 77
Football, 13, 14, 41–58, 59, 62
    homosexuals and, 43–46, 49, 57
Frenn, George, 131

Gallagher, Ed, 57–58
Gay and Lesbian March on Washington, 104
Gay Games, 21–23, 78, 79, 119, 127–28
    I, 21, 128–32
    II, 21, 132–36
    III, 21, 112, 136–38
    IV, 21, 23, 104, 138–39
    V, 21
Gay Softball League, 124
Gay Softball World Series, 124–25
Girls of Summer, The (Browne), 74
Golf, 31, 33–34
    homosexuals and, 31, 33
Goodstein, David, 19
Griffin, Pat, 26, 30, 34, 36

Haight, Abby, 38–39
Hayes, Bruce, 23, 109–12
Hockey, 49
Holleran, Andrew, 19, 20
Homophobia, 28, 37, 66, 123, 129

International Gay Bowling Organization, 126

International Gay Rodeo Association, 126

Jaynes, Betty, 30
Joyner-Kersee, Jackie, 28

Kamenshek, Dorothy, 77–78
Kaufman, Michelle, 13, 35
Kelly, Shawn, 134, 136, 138
King, Billie Jean, 33, 82, 90–98, 103, 104
Kinsey, Alfred, 15
Kopay, David, 13, 19, 20, 44–49, 50–57

Ladies Professional Golf Association (LPGA), 31, 33–34
League of Their Own, A (movie), 74
"Leagues of Their Own: Organized Responses to Sport Homophobia" (Pitts), 123–24
Lewinstein, Sara, 135
Lieberman, Nancy, 102, 103, 104
Louganis, Greg, 109

MacDonald, Douglas, 132
McGrievy, Susan, 131
McQueen, Robert, 121–23
Marshman, Don, 113–14
Maupin, Armistead, 132, 135, 136
Meisel, Barry, 20, 56, 57, 67
Menaker, Friedrich Engels "Enge," 114, 115, 116
Miller, Merle, 46
Mitchell, Jackie, 75
Myers, Joyce, 126

National Football League (NFL), 42, 44, 45, 46, 63
National Gay and Lesbian Bodybuilding Championships, 126
National Gay Softball Association, 124
National Hockey League (NHL), 49
National Lesbian and Gay Journalists Association, 38
Navratilova, Martina, 21, 31, 94, 98–105, 139
Nelson, Mariah Burton, 27, 28, 30, 31, 32, 34, 38, 128
North American Gay Amateur Athletic Alliance (NAGAAA), 124, 125

Odd Girls and Twilight Lovers (Faderman), 78
Olson, Greg, 126
Olympic Games, 15, 21, 47, 107–19
  1968, 21, 116–17, 119
  1984, 23, 111
Out, 33, 57

Paire, Lavonne "Pepper," 76, 77
Pallone, Dave, 70–73
Parsons, Pam, 25, 26, 27
Pitts, Brenda G., 123–24

Queer in America (Signorile), 19

Rosellini, Lynn, 20, 45, 46, 52
Rubyfruit Jungle (Brown), 100

Schaap, Dick, 84, 112, 136
"Silence So Loud It Screams, A" (Nelson), 31
Slattery, David, 49, 50, 53
Smith, Jerry, 45, 49, 50, 51, 52, 53, 54
Soccer, 58–59
  homosexuals and, 58
Softball, 78–79, 123, 124
Sports in America (Michener), 16–19
Steinberg, Alan, 73
Stonewall Riots, 130, 139

Team New York Aquatics, 112

Tennis, 81–105
  homosexuals and, 86
Tilden, William Tatem (Big Bill), 82–90
Title IX, 20, 27, 34
Toverud, Connie, 15–16

Underwood, Bob, 127

Waddell, Tom, 21, 23, 84, 109, 112–19, 127, 129, 132–36, 138, 139
Wilde, Oscar, 26
Wilson Report: Moms, Dads, Daughters and Sports, The, 26
Wisniewski, Connie, 77
Women's Basketball Coaches Association, 31
Women's Pro Basketball League, 27
Women's Tennis Association, 100

Young Men's Christian Association (YMCA), 33

Zaharias, Babe Didrikson, 33

Perry Deane Young, from Asheville, North Carolina, has worked as a journalist all over the world, including stints in Beirut in 1970 for the *New York Post* and in Vietnam in 1968 for United Press International. Besides writing for numerous national publications such as *Rolling Stone* and the *Advocate,* Young is the author of six nonfiction books. His book *The David Kopay Story,* named one of the ten best books of 1977 by the American Library Association, remained on the *New York Times* best-sellers list for nine weeks.

Martin Duberman is Distinguished Professor of History at the Graduate Center for the City University of New York and the founder and director of the Center for Gay and Lesbian Studies. One of the country's foremost historians, he is the author of 15 books and numerous articles and essays. He has won the Bancroft Prize for *Charles Francis Adams* (1960); two Lambda awards for *Hidden from History: Reclaiming the Gay and Lesbian Past,* an anthology that he coedited; and a special award from the National Academy of Arts and Letters for his overall "contributions to literature." His play *In White America* won the Vernon Rice/Drama Desk Award in 1964. His other works include *James Russell Lowell* (1966), *Black Mountain: An Exploration in Community* (1972), *Paul Robeson* (1989), *Cures: A Gay Man's Odyssey* (1991), and *Stonewall* (1993).

Professor Duberman received his Ph.D. in history from Harvard University in 1957 and served as professor of history at Yale University and Princeton University from 1957 until 1972, when he assumed his present position at the City University of New York.

PICTURE CREDITS